PRAISE FOR *BRAIN FIRST BUSINESS*

'Entrepreneurs with ADHD often feel like they're fighting their own brain while trying to build a company. Amanda shows them another way. *Brain First Business* is honest, practical, and deeply empowering. It will change how you work and how you lead.'

Gino Wickman, author of *Traction & Shine* and Creator of EOS®

'*Brain First Business* is the practical operating system for ADHD entrepreneurs. Amanda cuts through the noise and gives founders a clear, actionable framework to build a business that actually works for their brain.'

Ben Branson, founder of Seedlip & The Hidden 20%

'A wonderful reminder of the value of neurodiversity in business – and the vital need to amplify the remarkable rather than endlessly optimising the average. Never forget that the very same attributes that make you a bit of a pain on Monday morning can be a superpower on Friday afternoon.'

Rory Sutherland, author of *Alchemy* and vice-chairman of Ogilvy UK

'Traditional business advice is rooted in neurotypical thinking. This book challenges that entirely. As a founder, it highlights how to build in a way that aligns with how an ADHD brain works – validating, practical, and honestly game-changing.'

Laura Jackson, creative co-founder and creative director of Glassette and Rocco Beauty

BRAIN FIRST BUSINESS

Brain First Business

The ADHD Entrepreneur's Guide to Success

Amanda Perry

First published in Great Britain by John Murray Business in 2026
An imprint of John Murray Press

1

A CIP catalogue record for this title is available from the British Library

Trade Paperback ISBN 978 1 399 82900 7
ebook ISBN 978 1 399 82901 4

Typeset by KnowledgeWorks Global Ltd.

Printed and bound in Great Britain by Clays Ltd, Elcograf S.p.A.

John Murray Publishing Group policy is to use papers that are natural, renewable and recyclable products and made from wood grown in sustainable forests. The logging and manufacturing processes are expected to conform to the environmental regulations of the country of origin.

John Murray Publishing Group
Carmelite House
50 Victoria Embankment
London EC4Y 0DZ

John Murray Business
Hachette Book Group
123 South Broad Street
Ste 2750
Philadelphia, PA 19109, USA

www.johnmurraybusiness.com

John Murray Publishing Group, part of Hodder & Stoughton Limited
An Hachette UK company

The authorised representative in the EEA is Hachette Ireland, 8 Castlecourt Centre, Dublin 15, D15 XTP3, Ireland (email: info@hbgi.ie)

To my husband Steve,
without you none of this is possible.

Acknowledgements

Before I get into the main thank yous, I would like to thank my amazing community online, the ADHD trailblazer business owners, without whom this genuinely never would have happened. You are a constant source of support and guidance, cheering me on when things are good, cheering me up when things are bad, and holding me accountable when I get it wrong. It's easy to get caught up chasing the next shiny thing, but important to never forget who got you there. So thank you, this one is for all of you.

Ok, first and foremost I would like to thank my agent Jessica at The bks Agency for her hand-holding and appropriate pressure-for-the-situation pushing throughout this process. Thank you to Iain at John Murray Press in the UK and Emily at Hachette USA who have been beyond supportive from our very first meeting, and patient and kind with feedback, guiding me through every step of the way. And a special, huge thanks to Lynda, without whom there would possibly be no book to read!

Thank you to Laura Jackson, Lucy Menghini and Roei Samuel for sharing their journeys to be included in the book, and all the clients and community members who contributed too.

Thank you to my mum and dad for being gracious about me sharing my story – and in doing so, sharing theirs. Your support means the world to me.

Thank you to my friends who have been there – the ones who are authors and gave me practical support, the ones who are not and gave me emotional support, and everyone in between who just sent memes: thank you, I love you all.

Always last, but never, ever least – my wonderful husband, Steve, who never forgets bin day, never doubts me when I share another 'new idea' and opens all my mail for me. You are the glue that holds our family together and without you, truly, none of this is possible.

And finally to my gorgeous, cheeky, funny Baby A, everything I do is for you. You showed me what it means to live life and I promise to always play tickle monster in bed, kiss your hands better when you haven't hurt them and watch *Polar Express* with you non-stop from August.

A word on AI

In this book I discuss the use of AI and how I leverage it in my business. I think it's worth noting that this is an incredibly fast-moving technology which, along with the benefits, brings a whole raft of ethical and environmental concerns. At the time of writing this book, I do use it in certain areas of my business but am also acutely aware of the concerns around it and therefore urge you to use your own judgement when it comes to using it in your business.

Contents

PART III ACTION: Brain First you

Introduction

'Born to do it': ADHD, entrepreneurship and the importance of Brain First business

> **Business standards are neurotypical standards, 'fixing' yourself so you can achieve them is not the goal.**

The cliché of the hustle-hard founder who sells their possessions to pursue a vision that came to them overnight, sleeps on a mattress in their office and lives on nothing but ramen noodles might not be the lifestyle goal you or I aspire to ... but there's something we do have in common with that stereotype and that is (I'd bet on it) ADHD.

People with attention deficit hyperactivity disorder (ADHD) are around 70 per cent more likely to have entrepreneurial inclinations than our neurotypical (NT) counterparts, and we are twice as likely to actually start a business as someone who is neurotypical.[1] While official statistics estimate that 29 per cent of entrepreneurs have ADHD, it's also suggested that up to 85 per cent of people with ADHD are undiagnosed, or even unaware of this aspect of their identity.[2] If you're reading this book because you have, or suspect you have, ADHD, then that will be of little surprise as you'll already be aware of all the ways entrepreneurship appeals to an ADHD brain and why it's a much more compelling option than a clock-in/clock-out 9–5.

In theory, the many and varied traits of ADHD make us excellent entrepreneurs:

- Our creativity makes us natural solution-seekers and strategic thinkers.
- Our 'million ideas a minute' mean we are highly innovative and run ahead of the curve.
- Our high propensity to risk-take means we are more likely to jump and then learn to fly.
- Our ability to hyperfocus means we can work quickly to make things happen.

It can be easy to think of entrepreneurship as the perfect ADHD vehicle. However, the problem for us, and for those around us, is that if we build a business that relies on these attributes alone, then we end up in permanent burnout. Because for every trait that makes us an incredible entrepreneur, there are many that make us pretty terrible at business:

- We aren't great at attention to detail so can miss the finer points that, over time, can make or break a business.
- We get easily overwhelmed with admin tasks and can find seemingly basic business activities, like filling out forms, embarrassingly challenging.
- We are extremely prone to burnout, so while we can hyperfocus for a few hours, that is probably our energy for the day spent.

- We are poor planners due to the way we process time in 'now' or 'not now', and not great executors due to our executive functioning skills.
- Financial management can be difficult for us due to impulsivity and the way we process time, making it hard for us to forward plan.

I could go on.

This isn't your invite to a pity party, but if we are to claim our 'superpowers' and talk about being naturally gifted entrepreneurs, we have to be realistic about the parts that are hard for us too and that hold back so many talented and creative people from realising their business dreams.

So, what's going on? The ADHD connection

I don't know how I made it through 13 years of business before my diagnosis. I lurched from one crisis to another, partly because I wasn't compensating for my weaknesses and partly because I sabotaged any extended period of success (you know, just for a lil' extra dopamine kick).

Of course, I didn't know that at the time, so it was as frustrating for me as it was for those around me, and it led to many difficult conversations and disastrous corners to escape from – but I mostly coped. In fact, I thought that I was at my best when my back was against the wall. It turns out that I wasn't, I just didn't have a choice because I seemed to find myself there so often.

Far from being at my best, this way of doing business was actually causing long-term damage to my nervous system and mental health. I was surviving on the edge, abandoning my needs and putting everyone else in my business and life first – and I'm willing to bet many of you are doing exactly the same thing.

I have come to realise over the years that we ADHDers are *excellent* entrepreneurs: we can create the vision, have the ideas, get everyone excited and lead the charge. But when it comes to the business of business, we really aren't that great.

And guess what ... that's ok, so long as we recognise it.

In their book *Rocket Fuel*, Gino Wickman and Mark C Winters talk about how the essential combination in any business partnership is the mix of a visionary and an integrator. They even say that the visionary will often display 'ADHD traits'.[3]

Hearing this shortly after my diagnosis definitely shifted my whole mindset.

It finally helped me see that I wasn't a rubbish neurotypical who needed help from people, I was a brilliant, visionary neurodivergent (ND) entrepreneur who hadn't fully recognised the value I could bring. I always felt in the shadow of anyone who could do 'business' tasks like write a plan *and* follow it, or create a spreadsheet *and* fill it out every day. But I realised that my contribution was just as valid, if not more so. Without us, there is no business, no big picture to aim for, no disruption to the 'old way', and no innovation.

And in case you're thinking you can't have ADHD and succeed because you don't have a business partner – neither do I! The sense of empowerment for me came from realising my value and finally respecting the power of my brain. It allowed me to see that having the ideas, being creative and setting the vision is a whole role in and of itself. Go to any creative agency and they are the people paid the big bucks, revered by the whole agency – everyone else is just running round making it happen.

This isn't about the need for two people. It's about the need for you to recognise the power inside you and to start valuing yourself for the things you *can* do rather than judging yourself for the things you *can't*.

There is a quote that has been attributed to Henry Ford (you know, the guy that invented cars), which goes, 'If I listened to my customers, I would have invented a faster horse.'

I'm almost certain Ford never actually said this (but let's not worry about it). The phrase is often brought up to provide a counterpoint to the value of customer feedback in product design, but to me it tells a story of innovation. At a time of minimal technology (around the 1890s), this guy created something that previously didn't exist – where most people were perfectly happy with their horses, trotting around going about their daily business, he was dreaming up new ways to travel to the market.

Now, we are talking about more than 100 years before ADHD was even a diagnosable condition, so I'm not going to definitely say he had ADHD, but a quick Google search instantly reveals speculation from others[4] linking his abstract thinking (which led to him creating faster production lines and to mass produce cars) to the fact he could well have been in our neurodivergent club. He also had an apparent lack of focus for anything that didn't interest him ... sound familiar?

It would be great to think that things had changed significantly since Ford's time, but despite the noise in the media or the viral posts on LinkedIn highlighting the 1 per cent that are doing things differently, business really hasn't changed much since the 1950s when we transitioned from the industrial model to the corporate model.

In the industrial age, everything was about hierarchy – the bosses gave the orders and the workers followed them. Success was based on efficiency, conformity and obedience and was measured strictly in output, with no value placed on creativity or wellbeing. This was a business model built on structure.

From the 1950s that began to change as the post-war boom materialised into consumer demand and people's need for stability. Enter the corporate structure, as the 9–5 office job became the gold standard for a good life, where men left their picket-fenced houses to go to work and women stayed at home raising the children with the promise of a meal on the table as the father walked through the door.

This business model was built for *him*, and *he* was largely white, able bodied and – of course – neurotypical.

Around this time, the ground-breaking concept of 'management science' was introduced, with the core principle of *breaking every job into repeatable, measurable tasks and creating layers of managers to oversee productivity.*

Fast forward 75 years and honestly, not much has changed when we look at the bones of how we do business. While processes and key performance indicators (KPIs) were revolutionary back then, nearly a century later they have become over-optimised, over-valued and just another obstacle for a neurodivergent brain in modern business.

To run a business with ADHD is to permanently compromise yourself. You are either:

- sourcing energy that you don't have
- masking to present a persona that isn't you
- digging deep to do a task that your brain is fighting against
- internalising anxiety about almost every aspect of your business that feels entirely out of your control
- or holding your breath and getting through the day until you get home and close the door behind you so you can finally exhale.

I don't know about you, but if someone had sold the idea of running a business to me with those bullet points, I'm not sure that I would have jumped at the chance!

But rather than identifying the areas that are hardest for us, we are gaslit with traditional business advice that tells us:

- You just need to be consistent! (Could you please tell my underdeveloped prefrontal cortex that, because that guy hasn't got a consistent neuron to his name.)

- Outsource! Delegate! (ok, wonderful, I'll just use the energy I don't have from trying to wear all the hats, to communicate what I know needs doing, but don't know how to explain, to a stranger, shall I?)
- Dream big! (I do, that's kind of the problem.)
- Cash is king! (Yes, it is also the area of business I am most terrified of and have convinced myself will land me in prison the most often.)
- Have you tried writing it down? (Yes, I have. I even bought a notebook specifically for that purpose. Then forgot what 'it' was.)

Well, the time for change is here and building a Brain First business is how we will do it. Because while every business needs to be clear on the destination, we can all choose to take a different route to get there.

My Brain First journey: Understanding and accepting my ADHD identity

I recently found some of my reports from school (I won't linger on this too much as I know you could also write this next line) and they were all some version of:

> Amanda shows great potential, if only she could focus/stop distracting others/concentrate in class/stop being the class clown.

Reading them was a surprisingly emotional experience. I really didn't expect to cry – I have seen them a hundred times and could have told you what each one said without ever seeing them again in my life – but on this occasion, reading them for the first time since my diagnosis in 2020, they hit different.

We all know that pre-diagnosis it felt like we were doing life in hard mode, and we were never quite sure why. In fact, there is a stat that says that by the time they are ten, neurodivergent children will have been exposed to 20,000 more negative messages than their neurotypical counterparts.[5]

TWENTY THOUSAND!

That equates to five more negative messages a day than your friend who doesn't have a neurodevelopmental condition. And we wonder why we have a fragile sense of self and shattered self-esteem as adults.

And that is a modern statistic, based on kids who have been diagnosed and live in a time when there is more understanding around this stuff (I know, still not enough, but in comparison to when my generation were at school, we are talking light years ahead). Imagine the impact that had on our brain as we went about our day thinking we were just like everyone else.

Having worked with hundreds of neurodivergent adults, I have seen first hand the impact these formative years had on them and it breaks my heart ... because it had the same impact on me. It's what drives me to make a change to the way we do things, to open our eyes to the fact that business standards are neurotypical standards, and to address the lack of deeper understanding when it comes to advocating for ourselves in the business world. Because those neurotypical standards are what make this shit hard.

I write this book now as a mid-40s female entrepreneur, who has been in business for 18 years and in that time has experienced success and awards and praise and accolades and also failure and bankruptcy and heartache and trauma. And I'm 100 per cent sure that if I knew then what I know now, it would have been a very different story.

As it was, I started out in 2007 leaving my successful corporate job to follow the dream of owning a cupcake business. Even though I upped the challenge level by opening during a deep recession, over the next seven years we grew to seven shops and more than 100 staff.

By 2014, however, I was burnt out and the business was bankrupt. It was one of the most difficult times in my life (I'll tell you more about it as the book goes on – it's not just about sharing the highs). For the following few years I experimented with different business ideas. Some worked and some didn't, but they led me to a new venture – this time offering marketing support to other businesses. Over the next five years, I took that from a freelance gig to a full agency with 40 staff.

I sold the agency in 2022, a decision influenced in no small part by my ADHD diagnosis in 2020.

It's hard to describe the ADHD diagnosis journey to someone who hasn't been through it. We usually associate the term 'diagnosis' with something bad, but with ADHD – certainly for me – it felt like the best news I had ever received in my life.

Ok, let me break that down a bit because that's not strictly true. I remember walking out of my assessment feeling faint and dizzy. And as you will know if you have been through diagnosis or discovery, what followed was the grief/relief cycle for a good six months as I made peace with 'what could have been' and spent time with the flashing montage of my life playing back as I made sense of its key moments.

But ultimately, my diagnosis brought about a clarity that I just couldn't ignore, and the more I understood my brain, the more I realised that rather than building a business, I had built a mental and physical prison.

The daily toll on my brain was too much to take. I was in permanent sensory overload from people and noise, and my brain was drained from over-extending my executive function capabilities every day for the past 13 years.

Because that's the thing about being neurodivergent: once you know, you can't ignore it.

It took me 18 months to finally admit to myself that things were not working for me and to make the change that I so desperately needed. Selling my agency definitely wasn't the easy option – there were a ton of moving parts to consider, including clients, team members and other commitments, but I knew that if I didn't make the change, it would be too late, and my health was too big a price to pay. I could finally see, with crystal-clear vision, exactly how I wanted my business to look, feel and run, and for the first time I knew I could make it happen because I was finally operating from a place of awareness. And that felt so good.

This started a process of reshaping my professional life so that it worked for me and not the other way round – effectively the beginning of the 'Brain First' thinking you're going to hear so much about here. Since then, I've concentrated on helping other ADHD entrepreneurs understand what they need to thrive and how they can go about achieving their goals (without losing themselves in the process).

Your Brain First business: The basics

I have often said I wouldn't change the past because it's led me to where I am today, which makes for a great line on a podcast or in the press, but there is so much nuance to that.

Do I have regrets? Actually, yeah, I do. I regret a lot of things I have done, and I deeply regret the fact that I didn't know I had ADHD and so couldn't understand myself better and accommodate for my needs.

Would I change the past? I would definitely change parts of it. I'd change the bits where I neglected myself and damaged my mental health to prove ... something, to ... someone. I'd change the bits where I hurt others because I didn't understand that I was dysregulated and so couldn't moderate my emotions or behaviours.

Am I also proud of who I am today? Yes. I can finally say I am.

The mindset shift gifted to me by Wickman and Winters led me on the path to creating a business that not just values my brain but puts it at the centre of every decision and opportunity that comes my way.

I call this a Brain First business.

I want this book to help you create a business that values *your* brain and puts *your* brain at the centre of everything you do. I want you to understand that business doesn't have to look one way – you can create your business, in your vision, and achieve your truest dreams, without compromising your sanity in the process.

Business standards are neurotypical standards, so if you are an ADHD entrepreneur battling against the tide, then this book is the permission slip you need to create your business your way.

The Brain First method will encourage you to reconsider everything you know about business. It will invite you to rebuild yours from the ground up, putting your brain before your customers, clients or stakeholders. Think that sounds selfish? It's actually the least selfish thing you can do and I can't wait to show you why.

This book will help you reframe what success means to you, how you choose to go about achieving it and how to enjoy the journey along the way. No cookie-cutter recipe, just a much-needed reset and new approach to business that will help you see how achievable your goals really are.

THE BRAIN FIRST METHOD: THE PATHWAY TO YOUR BRAIN FIRST SUCCESS

Ok, are you ready? Let's get into this.

As much as this book isn't business-by-numbers (for many reasons, partly because having ADHD means we hate being told what to do!), there is a method and a framework for you to follow as you build your Brain First business. This method has been distilled from my years of business coaching (with both neurotypical and neurodivergent clients) and from working with hundreds of ADHD business owners to help them get out of the burnout-by-bullying cycle.

You know that cycle! It's the one where we start a business by grabbing hold of a creative spark that hits us at 3 am and just won't leave. We jump in with both feet and LOVE what we do, but slowly, over time, and as we start to feel like more of a business, we absorb the messaging around us – about how we 'should' be doing things, how 'they' do things and what will happen if we don't do things that way (spoiler alert: it ain't pretty!).

And so we start getting tough with ourselves. It starts off fairly mildly (as most bullying does), but before long we are calling ourselves names so awful that we didn't even hear them in the playground. We start to feel the pressure.

Long gone is the gut instinct we used to trust so confidently, and no matter how much we try to tune in, all we hear is that voice inside mocking us for thinking we have the answers and telling us that business isn't done by gut, it's done by spreadsheets and KPIs.

Well, if we're going to continue on this journey together then I need you to promise me one thing: I'm not going to ask you to break up with the bully just yet – I know it's going to take more than a few pages of a book to break that special bond – but I am going to ask you to start noticing when they speak up and recognising that it's not your voice ... and it's lying to you.

You AREN'T useless.

You DO know what you're doing.

You HAVEN'T just 'fluked' it.

And you DO deserve success.

Instead, this is the point when I need you to really process that business standards are neurotypical standards and as long as we continue to bully ourselves into working to them (or try to look to the rest of the world as though we are), we will continue on the burnout-by-bullying cycle and will never find our true, soul-satisfying, full-life living, money-making, joyous business.

You know, the one you dreamt of when you started? Let's create THAT version!

THE METHOD

This won't be the last time you hear me say this in this book, but it's really important to remember that ADHD isn't a personality type and if you have met one person with ADHD, you have literally met one person with ADHD.

I have worked with enough ADHD business owners to know that my version of a Brain First business would be their idea of hell, and vice versa. Working with ADHD is a personal journey because, as with most neurodivergent conditions, symptoms and traits show up in each of us as a spectrum. You might be dialled up on the inattentive side and struggle with conceptualising time, whereas someone else may struggle more with demand avoidance and how to focus their energy.

This is all to say that this isn't a 'one size fits all' roadmap but a path to follow that will give each of you a completely different result, based on your unique brain – so although you will be reading the same book, you will all land on completely different Brain First plans and businesses.

In each chapter in the 'Your Brain First business' section, you'll find strategies and advice that you can tailor to your own situation, enabling you to build a personal toolkit of go-to guidance for whatever challenge you're facing at the time. These toolkit elements, including exercises to help you plan for your own business, can also be downloaded from http://book.brainfirst.co. Take your time to complete the exercises as you go, as each chapter jumps off from the previous one. By the time you finish the book, you will have finished your toolkit too and will have developed a whole new way of doing business.

The absolute joy of this is that there's no way for you to do better or worse than anyone, to be left behind, or to feel that this book is another thing you read and then did nothing with (I see you).

The Brain First method is less a three-step plan, more a three-step invitation to take the time to truly understand yourself and reach a point of acceptance, to view your business through that new lens of acceptance and self-compassion, and to identify the changes that MUST be made and (brace yourself for this one) put yourself first as you go through the process of implementing them.

This isn't about throwing the baby out with the bathwater either, it's about enjoying the process of discovery, going at your own pace, taking a few steps forward and a few back – perhaps even a few to the side from time to time.

It's a self-paced fun run – NOT a marathon.

Because the truth is, until you do embrace this new way of business, you will continue to bully yourself through that burnout cycle and are unlikely to ever reach your version of success, and certainly not sustainably. I can promise you that from personal experience (more on that story later).

The three steps you need to understand at this stage are shown in the figure.

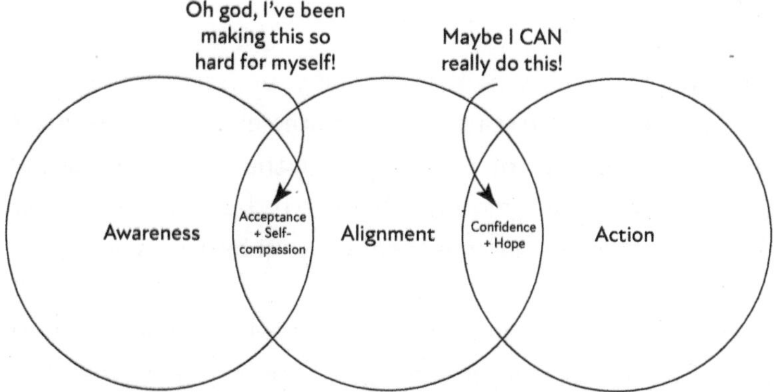

1. AWARENESS

You are probably here. Step one is about understanding ADHD and how it shows up in you. Remember, we are not the same and so learning about how your brain works is the key to moving forward with acceptance and self-compassion. In this book I help you to do that through a deep understanding of ADHD and reflecting on how you experience it.

2. ALIGNMENT

Once you have really understood just how much ADHD impacts you and your business (and I mean really understood, like, I need to see tears!), we can start looking at your business through THAT lens (rather than the lens of the LinkedIn bro who is telling you that you don't have a business unless you're travelling in first class and starting work at 5 am *vomit emoji*). I help you through that in the book by imagining what your business could look like – we can't be what we can't see, so let me help you see it.

3. ACTION

Once we have a clear picture of what your Brain First business will look like, we can start finding strategies and tools to make that happen. I help you through this in the book by looking at the most common symptoms that trip us up and how you can work with them or reframe them to work best for you.

Exercises to help you understand yourself and your business better, as well as customisable guidance, appear in the 'Your Brain First business' sections at the end of each chapter and are designed to become a toolkit that you can refer to whenever you need. All toolkit resources can also be downloaded from http://book.brainfirst.co.

All you need right now is an open mind and a desire to make your life easier.

REFRAMING WHAT YOU THOUGHT YOU KNEW

Without you there is no business. Without you, there was no idea that then became a week-long Google search, that then became a business name, that then became a 'let's give it a go', that then became something that paid your bills and took your family on holiday, that then paid other people so they could pay their bills and take their family on holiday too.

Business, and progress, need us – and we have so much to give. We just need to find a way to work that leans into our strengths first, then everyone wins.

TL;DR

The business model introduced in the 1950s was for (white, able-bodied) *neurotypical* men – and it hasn't changed since then.

The Brain First method isn't about compromising on your goals; it's about achieving them by design. You are brilliant, but you need to accept that while you can do anything, you can't do everything.

Realising your worth and understanding the value you bring to your business and those around you is the first step towards creating the business that you deserve and that your brain needs.

PART I
Awareness
Starting out

Your guide to Part I

Part I, Awareness, is a foundational step in building your Brain First business, so even if you think you know everything about ADHD, I urge you not to skip it.

Our general awareness around ADHD and neurodivergence has developed dramatically in recent years – and continues to do so – but when it comes to understanding how your unique brain interacts with the world, we have some work to do. This Part is all about inviting you to do that work, with someone by your side the whole way.

Over the following chapters, I will take you through some of the key challenges with ADHD in business and we'll take a look at what is really going on in your brain to give you a deeper understanding of your own needs. This should feel like a permission slip for you to build your business *your* way.

It was never about trying harder, or focusing more, or paying attention – it was the way you were born.

And now, one gift to you before we begin.

In my never-ending pursuit to distil the ADHD experience into a simple, concise soundbite (or eye-bite, as it's turned out in book form), I took inspiration from Maslow's Hierarchy of Needs[6] and created what I have imaginatively called the ADHD Hierarchy of Energy Needs (see below). This simple visual shows exactly what we need, in the order we need it, to stand the best chance of harnessing the energy we need to focus.

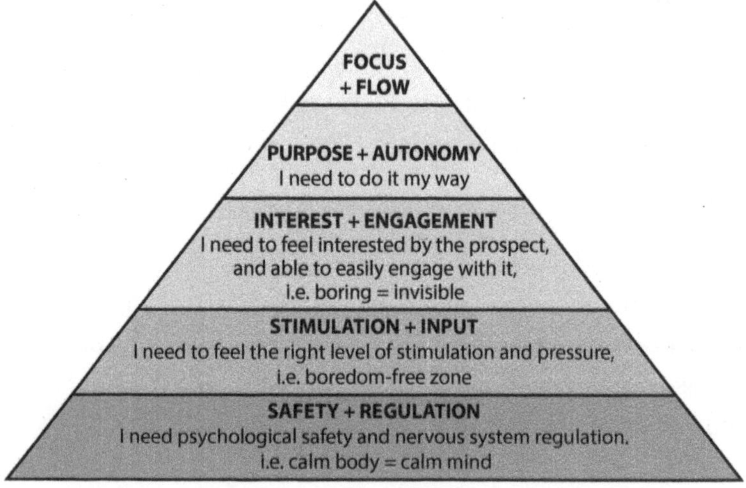

I am sharing this with you here because it's pretty foundational to everything we are about to dig into, so here you go – feel free to highlight, turn down the page, take a picture, get a tattoo ... whatever works for you to build it into your daily practice and remember it FOR EVER.

1

Awareness is power

Understanding the ADHD brain

> ADHD is less about not knowing what to do and more about struggling to do it consistently – especially if it's boring, stressful or not immediately rewarding.

Before we jump in feet first – you know, the way we do – let's take a moment and make sure we're all on the same page in terms of our understanding of ADHD because you have to understand *the* ADHD brain in order to understand *your* ADHD brain.

As anyone with ADHD will know, thanks to algorithms, as soon as you have so much as looked in the direction of an ADHD meme, your feed will be flooded with a range of content – from science-backed expert advice to lived-experience 'storytimes' to relatable quotes and shares, all with one objective in mind: engagement.

Something that started off as a way for people to find others who understood them quickly turned into a commercial opportunity and the lines got kind of blurred. In fact, in 2021, the University of British Columbia ran a study of the top 100 performing videos under the hashtag ADHD according to likes and views and assessed each of them. In the study, 52 per cent were classified as misleading, 27 per cent as personal experience and just 21 per cent as useful.[7]

And this is why it's so important to understand the facts – as far as we know them – about our brain. It's easy to get caught up in a dopamine deluge of funny memes or comforting lived experience stories. These all have their place but are no replacement for truly understanding how your own brain works so that you can finally make friends with it and work together.

I also think it's important to know some of the science behind ADHD to shut down the voice that still pipes up from time to time questioning if you really are just a bit lazy or looking for an excuse. Just to be really clear on this, I am not a scientific expert and I don't have any letters after my name. But what I do have is years of research in this area, so I'm going to share with you the things I have learnt that I think are most important to understand about the ADHD brain when building your Brain First business.

So, what's going on? The ADHD connection

1. ADHD is a neurodevelopmental condition, which means the brain develops differently, especially in areas that manage attention, emotions, time and self-control.

2. ADHD is a largely genetic condition, meaning it runs in families (how many of us took a good look around us when we got our diagnosis?), roughly breaking down like this:
   - Parent with ADHD: child has a 40–60 per cent chance of also having ADHD.
   - Siblings of someone with ADHD: 20–35 per cent increased likelihood.
   - Identical twin with ADHD: the other twin has a 60–90 per cent chance of also having it. (Although the heritability rate is around 70–84 per cent, environmental factors such as prenatal exposure to alcohol or drugs and childhood trauma can also trigger or intensify symptoms.[8])

   This matters because how many of us have carried the 'should have tried harder' guilt around since reading those school reports, or watched as our peers fly up the corporate ladder or sweep the awards and accolades for their business? Well, you can stop that right now – it's the brain you were blessed with from birth.
3. The ADHD brain has impaired activity in four functional regions of the brain:
   - prefrontal cortex (responsible for executive function, focus and organisation)
   - limbic system (regulates our emotions)
   - basal ganglia (where inter-brain communication *should* happen)
   - reticular activating system (the bouncers in your brain filtering incoming sensory information – impairment here leads to inattention, impulsivity or hyperactivity).
4. The human brain relies on seven major networks to keep us alive, all responsible for their own thing, ranging from movement to decision-making to regulating our

emotions. Out of the seven major brain networks, three are impacted by ADHD:

- Default mode network (DMN): responsible for mind-wandering and daydreaming, this is the network responsible for what's happened when you drive to your destination and have no idea how you got there. While part of the brain is taking care of business (and managing the car), the DMN is the part that's off on a flight of fancy about whether starting up a business selling ice cream on the beach really *would* be a good idea. In our ADHD brain, the DMN often stays too active – even when we want to put all our concentration elsewhere.
- Task positive network (TPN): this one is in charge of focus and attention. In a neurotypical brain it will know how to stay on-task until the job is complete. In our brain, it just can't stay engaged as easily, especially if the task isn't stimulating.
- Salience network: this is the system that chooses which network to switch to. It is meant to choose a network based on priorities or importance – for example, to pivot from the default mode when we're thinking of new ideas to the task positive network when we need to figure out how to turn our ideas into action – but in our brain it struggles to decide which task is most important and then struggles to make the switch.

5. You may have heard of dopamine, which is a chemical that the body uses to communicate between nerve cells. It's particularly connected to our experience of reward and motivation – when we do something we like, the body releases dopamine into our system, enhancing

the good feeling (reward) and causing us to repeat the behaviour to get the feeling again (motivation). What you may have heard less about is the related neurotransmitter and hormone norepinephrine (*nu-rep-eh-neff-ren*), which also has a big role to play in ADHD. Norepinephrine is produced from dopamine and it helps our brain regulate attention, impulse control and focus, as well as being a major player in our fight or flight response – all key to the ADHD experience. Stimulant (and non-stimulant) medications are prescribed to increase levels of norepinephrine in the brain in order to improve focus and attention.

Because norepinephrine comes from dopamine, you can naturally increase levels through diet and nutrition by focusing on dopamine-rich foods like chocolate (yay!), nuts and eggs. Alternatively, you can stock up on vegetables like broccoli and cauliflower, which are great sources of chromium (believed to play a key role in norepinephrine production).

6. There are increasingly high rates of co-occurrence of neurodivergent conditions and research that suggests it's far more prevalent than once thought. The DSM-5 (the medical reference for mental health and brain-related conditions) was only revised in 2013 to allow for autism and ADHD to be diagnosed together, but some current estimates have presentation rates of ADHD and autism together (often referred to as AuDHD) being as high as 75 per cent.[9] This is important because in order to have awareness of our brain, it helps to have the correct 'label'.

But what does all of this tell us?

ADHD is part of us, we're born with it – it's not something we develop. While a neurotypical brain is able to more easily focus on 'important things', do things because 'they need to be done' or delay gratification in a task, our ADHD brain struggles because our nervous system is wired to seek stimulation and avoid boredom in order to self-regulate dopamine and feel balanced. Sitting down and just getting something done because it should be done runs counter to all our instincts.

That is why motivation drivers in the ADHD brain are only activated by these four things: interest, novelty, competition and urgency (INCU). To elaborate:

- Interest: do I actually care about that task/event/idea in front of me – like, does it give me tingles? Because if not, it ain't happening!
- Novelty: is this something that feels new and exciting? Even if it's not the first time doing something and is just a new approach, novelty will kick our brain into action.
- Competition: some like to use challenge in place of this one – either way, gamifying the process is almost guaranteed to get us there.
- Urgency: this is the ultimate kick-up-the-bum. If we are trying to do a task without that sense of 'oh-my-god-if-I-don't-do-this-now-then-there-will-be-consequences', it's unlikely we will get it done.

We'll come back to INCU throughout the book, but for now just remember: ADHD is less about not knowing what to do and more about struggling to do it consistently – especially if it's boring, stressful or not immediately rewarding.

My Brain First journey: The first business

There is no better way for me to explain the impact ADHD can have than sharing some of my experience.

My business journey started in 2007 – in fact, the day I handed in my notice to my corporate job was the day people were queuing around the block of UK bank Northern Rock to get their money out. If you're old enough, you will know that was the start of the 2007 credit crunch, which lasted well into 2009. People thought I was crazy leaving a secure, well-paid job to make cupcakes from home just as the worst recession since the Great Depression in 1929 was unfolding.

Obviously at that point I didn't know quite how bad things would get, but even if I had, it wouldn't have changed my mind. I had a vision, no dependants and a £29 hand whisk from the supermarket ... hyperfocus was LOCKED IN. I was still in my 20s (just), undiagnosed and blissfully unaware of the ways my brain would lull me into a false sense of security over the next six years – innovating and disrupting with ease, but planning and measuring with absolute avoidance. I jumped into that business with both feet, both hands and every other body part, racing towards each goal, as amazed as anyone around me at what a success I had become.

Despite the recession hitting hard, I managed to weather the storm and build that business from a £29 piece of kitchen equipment to seven shops, over 100 staff and an annual turnover of £1 million over five years. I am so proud of what I achieved and so grateful for the lessons I learnt ... but my God, it took its toll.

The strengths I took into that business were overshadowed by a lack of awareness of my weaknesses, and by the time they became apparent, it was really too late. I had people in positions of responsibility to support me, but even that dynamic was difficult to manage and just added to the chaos. I remember meetings where I was trying to focus on a spreadsheet someone would be taking me through line by line – the numbers would just be swimming around in front of my eyes, impossible to focus on, but I didn't have the words to explain why. How could I say to someone who was doing their job that I couldn't concentrate on the important information they were sharing with me because it was boring and repetitive?

Thank goodness now I know so much more about the strengths of ADHD and that I feel more comfortable sharing the weaknesses. But when you don't know that your brain works differently, how can you explain it to someone else? It's an impossible situation that can only lead to burnout.

Despite not being diagnosed for another five years after that business breathed its last, I left it with a very clear idea of what worked and what didn't work for me. Although they were lessons I would have to learn a few more times before I finally understood that ignoring them and *trying harder* wasn't the solution. Awareness, alignment and action were the only answer.

Your Brain First business: Understanding where you are on your Brain First journey

If you've lived your life with undiscovered ADHD, it's all too easy to continue gaslighting yourself, even after you have a bit of paper making your diagnosis official. Maybe I just gave really good answers at the clinical assessment? Maybe I've just watched too many TikToks and now I'm using this as an easy excuse for my own mistakes? And so it goes on.

Let's just insert the record scratch sound effect here and stop you right there – ADHD is real, you're not pretending, and now you have the science to back up that it is literally how your brain is wired. The messages you have absorbed and internalised around being lazy or flaky aren't true and we are going to proceed with that understanding – deal?

With that in mind, let's take a moment to assess where you are on your Brain First journey. As you do this remember that it's not about achieving a perfect score – you won't be scoring 4s and 5s on everything (anything!), so don't let the self-doubt gremlin creep in. This is about being honest so you can get a better sense of areas that are working and so you can dive into what isn't. And if nothing is working, well, it's a good thing you are reading this book.

Instructions: Rate each statement from 1 to 5:

1 = Never | 2 = Rarely | 3 = Sometimes | 4 = Often | 5 = Always

Keep a track of your score so you can review it at the end of each section.

1. Energy & Capacity

Statement	1	2	3	4	5
I structure my day around my natural energy levels					
I take breaks before I feel overwhelmed or burnt out					
I've built in recovery time after intense work periods					
I can recognise the signs that I'm pushing beyond my limits					
I don't rely on caffeine and stress to power through the day					

Total Score for Energy & Capacity: ________

2. Focus & Task Management

Statement	1	2	3	4	5
I have a system that helps me start and finish tasks effectively					
I don't rely on last-minute pressure to get things done					
I can break down tasks into manageable steps when I feel overwhelmed					
I regularly get to the end of the day having completed what matters most					
I have strategies for getting back on track after distraction or derailment					

Total Score for Focus & Task Management: ________

3. Time & Structure

Statement	1	2	3	4	5
I have a consistent daily or weekly rhythm that supports my brain					
I give myself time buffers between tasks or meetings					
I know how long things really take – and plan accordingly					
My calendar reflects what actually matters, not just what's urgent					
I can shift gears without feeling mentally scrambled or stressed					

Total Score for Time & Structure: ________

4. Environment & Tools

Statement	1	2	3	4	5
My workspace feels calm, clear and suits how I like to work					
I use digital or physical tools that help me stay organised					
I minimise distractions in my physical and digital environments					
My workspace supports my sensory needs (e.g. sound, light, comfort)					
I can easily find what I need when I need it					

Total Score for Environment & Tools: ________

5. Support & Delegation

Statement	1	2	3	4	5
I don't try to do everything myself					
I regularly ask for support, through people, systems or tech					
I know which tasks I shouldn't be doing myself					
I use accountability systems (e.g. co-working, coaching, automation) to help me follow through					
I have people or processes that catch things when I drop the ball					

Total Score for Support & Delegation: ________

6. Emotional Regulation

Statement	1	2	3	4	5
I can recover fairly quickly from emotional dips or setbacks					
I know what triggers over-whelm, shutdown or rejection sensitivity					
I have tools that help me regulate when I feel dysregulated					
I don't beat myself up for needing rest or moving slowly					
I feel emotionally safe inside my business					

Total Score for Emotional Regulation: ________

7. Alignment & Purpose

Statement	1	2	3	4	5
I regularly feel excited or energised by my work					
I've built my business around my strengths, not around what others expect					
I say no to things that don't align with my energy, values or focus					
I'm not trying to run a 'neurotypical business'					
My business feels like it's growing with me, not draining me					

Total Score for Alignment & Purpose: ________

Your Brain First Score:

101–175: You've got this nailed! This book will help you refine and improve what you're currently doing.
51–100: You've got some things in place, but this book will help you fall in love with your business again.
0–50: You're working against your brain and making it so hard for yourself ... you're going to love this book.

Reframing what you thought you knew

Understanding the science backs up the fact that you are swimming against a tide that you can't beat using neurotypical techniques. Now that you understand this, you can start to release the layers of conditioning that have impacted you throughout your life and begin to operate from a place of kindness and self-compassion.

Think about the reason you are in business in the first place: it might be to provide for your family, for flexibility to travel, to prove yourself to your English teacher or even to change the world. How well can you fulfil any of those things if you carry on 'pushing through' the way you currently are? Lurching from one week to the next with the promise of 'things will ease up soon', masking your way through the hard times and never fully enjoying the good because your mind is racing on to the next challenge, trying to do business the 'proper' way?

I get it. I have lived it – and I still do sometimes, until I remind myself that there are other, better ways. And that I need to find them to fulfil my 'why' (in my case, this is to give my son the life he deserves).

So, take this as your reframe: putting your brain at the centre of everything you do in your business isn't selfish ... if it keeps you afloat, it will keep others afloat too. It's actually the least selfish thing you can do.

I truly believe that individualisation (that is, shaping your business around your individual needs) is at the heart of future business success – for everyone. But it's even more important for us, and if we are to build a level playing field to success and catch up with those who had the user manual all along, then it feels only right that we get a chance to nail this first.

TL;DR

ADHD is a neurodevelopmental and largely genetic condition affecting brain regions responsible for attention, emotions and self-control.

It impacts three major brain networks (the default mode network, the task positive network and the salience network), making it hard to switch focus or stay on task.

While ADHD is often linked to low dopamine, norepinephrine is also key in regulating attention and impulse control. Medication and diet can help by boosting norepinephrine levels.

2

A life of questions

Undoing old traumas

> **The trauma of living with undiagnosed ADHD in a world that wasn't made for me is much more damaging than the trauma of living with a brain that is wired differently.**

Just before we get into this chapter, I need you to know that I am not a therapist. The reason I decided to cover this topic is because I believe a key part of becoming aware is being able to pull apart the behaviours that are linked to our neurodivergent brain from the ones that are patterns we have developed as a trauma response to growing up with a neurodivergent brain. If this chapter raises feelings and emotions that you find difficult to process, please speak to a professional for support.

Anyone living with a neurodivergent brain knows that we experience our differences in many ways. This is particularly true if you are late-diagnosed/late-recognised and have spent the majority of your life wondering why things seem to feel so much harder for you than they appear to feel for others, or being treated differently by teachers or family members.

I'm sure we all have stories from our childhood that stand out – and have possibly been repeated to therapists over the years – that make sense now we understand more about our brain. Not everyone is ready to accept this, but those stories that are often trotted out over the family dinner table – like the time you left your exam early because you were finished, only to realise you hadn't turned the paper over to read the ESSAY TOPIC of the back of the sheet ... you know the kind of thing – are all examples of ADHD-related trauma.

Trauma is a funny thing (very much not in the LOL sense) and we are often reluctant to label something as traumatic when it happens to us but quick to recognise it in others.

Let me tell you a story. I must have been around 12 when I remember going to a swimming lesson in secondary school. These were held at the leisure centre, just a short walk from the school. Being a chubby teenage girl with excruciating anxiety at the thought of being in a swimming costume in front of my classmates, I would do everything I could to minimise the pain. This included sneaking off to the toilets in advance to change into my costume, just to save the embarrassment of changing in the locker room with the group.

In my haste to avoid any embarrassment, I had changed into my swimsuit, put my uniform back over the top and left school with the rest of the class – blissfully unaware until the lesson ended that I had forgotten to take my underwear with me.

Don't ask me why, but this caused a disproportionate response from me, which included tears. My (on reflection, very unempathetic) PE teacher was alerted and decided that the only solution was to make me walk back from the pool to school in just my swimming costume, wrapped in a towel that didn't meet in the middle – past 'smokers' tree', the school tennis courts and through the maths block. Everything.

It was excruciating. Every terrifying step reinforced all the awful things I believed about myself at such a young age: I was stupid, I couldn't even remember simple things, I was never going to be good enough. Every time someone pointed, laughed or shouted a name at me, it turned those thoughts into fact.

It took a therapist some 20 years later to name that experience as trauma – and still I didn't believe her. I believed trauma to be abuse, neglect or death. Not a silly little walk from a silly little swimming pool for something that was my own silly fault.

Just to be clear here, in case you aren't aware, in therapy they talk about two types of trauma:

- big T trauma: abuse, neglect, death, major life-changing moments
- little t trauma: emotionally distressing events that aren't life-changing moments but cause significant emotional and psychological damage.

You will have your own version of my swimming pool story, your own experiences of trauma, caused by living in a world that wasn't designed for your brain. And this isn't just a childhood thing – if our childhood is the foundation of our traumatised nervous system, then the continuation into adulthood, without any upgrade to our operating system (i.e. a diagnosis or recognition of our differences), becomes a version of my toddler's Duplo towers: messy, unstable and unlikely to withstand much pressure.

I don't know about you, but personally I find it's not my ADHD that causes me distress – it's living in a world that doesn't recognise my needs.

So, what's going on? The ADHD connection

I think of trauma a bit like those Spirograph games we used to play with as kids where the longer you draw for, the more the lines connect, and overlap, and patterns develop. In fact, as ADHD symptoms can so closely mimic those of Post Traumatic Stress Disorder (PTSD) and Complex Post Traumatic Stress Disorder (cPTSD), it's common for misdiagnosis to occur.

According to research on the topic, adults with ADHD have a significantly elevated risk of developing PTSD/cPTSD, with prevalence of comorbidity between 28 per cent and 36 per cent[10] (estimates put rates of PTSD in the general population in the UK at any one time at 4 in 100, or 4 per cent).[11]

Here's why ADHD and PTSD/cPTSD can be hard to pick apart:

- Women with ADHD are more likely to have a history of developmental trauma and are more likely to be under-diagnosed or misdiagnosed with mood or personality disorders before ADHD is recognised.
- Both ADHD and PTSD/cPTSD show impairments in executive functioning, including planning, memory and emotional regulation. This would take a super in-depth and long-term assessment to understand in an individual. Unfortunately, that isn't the way we are commonly diagnosed.

- Chronic stress and trauma can alter the prefrontal cortex and the HPA axis (the hypothalamic-pituitary-adrenal axis, which is a hormonal system that helps the body manage stress), both of which are already affected in ADHD brains.
- Emotional dysregulation is a core feature of both, but in ADHD it's neurological, while in PTSD/cPTSD it's often trauma-adaptive.
- Shame and self-doubt from undiagnosed ADHD can become traumatic in themselves, especially if a person was persistently punished, scapegoated or misunderstood while growing up.

This is so important when we start to look at how we run our businesses because until we understand not just the immediate ways ADHD impacts us (our strengths and weaknesses) but also those behaviour patterns and trauma responses that have become an ingrained part of our personality, we will struggle to move past the cycles we are currently repeating – and are desperate to break.

- Perhaps you were called lazy as a kid so struggle to ask for help now because it feels too vulnerable.
- Perhaps you were told by a teacher you'd never amount to anything so you run your business in 'prove mode' now, pushing yourself to the edges of burnout every time.
- Perhaps you got bullied at school so find it hard to trust people now and end up doing everything yourself.
- Perhaps the (big or little t) trauma you experienced left you hypervigilant so now, no matter how good things get, you're always on high alert waiting for it to go wrong.

If you are going to build a Brain First business – one that recognises every facet of what makes you *you*, and is designed to work for you on every level – then it's important that you take the time to not only recognise obvious things that impact your day-to-day but dig a little deeper too.

Let's set aside all our limitations and imagine that this is the start of you building your hyper-personalised business which will serve you for ever – because it is.

ADHD is essentially a nervous system regulation condition, not just a focus issue. So our biggest challenge becomes maintaining a regulated status – and too many of us don't even know what that feels like because we're so used to living in fight, flight or freeze mode.

Our brain is wired to seek stimulation, our stress response is often heightened, and we're more likely to experience emotional intensity and rejection sensitivity. So our baseline is already more *sensitive* to the environment than a neurotypical person's would be.

Trauma (whether it's big T or little t trauma) activates the sympathetic nervous system: our fight/flight response. If this activation happens repeatedly or isn't resolved, your system can become stuck in a state of hypervigilance or shutdown. This can look like:

- constantly scanning for danger
- feeling 'on edge' or easily overwhelmed
- difficulty calming down or relaxing
- trouble trusting yourself or others
- burnout and exhaustion because your body is burning through energy trying to keep you 'safe'.

When you consider that we are more likely to experience trauma because we grew up in a world that wasn't designed for us, with no understanding about our brain, and likely surrounded by other dysregulated, undiagnosed and unaware family members, then it's no wonder we adopt these survival strategies and they just become, well, who we are.

When trauma is presented on top of ADHD it can significantly increase symptoms and make something that is tricky to manage almost impossible. Someone who is distracted could switch between hypervigilance and disassociating (which is the experience of feeling detached from reality); someone who is impulsive might become reactively defensive or focus their impulsivity on more dopamine-seeking, dangerous behaviour; and even day to day you might notice that procrastination, rejection sensitivity and distraction increase to a point that they feel almost impossible to manage.

My Brain First journey: Building my trauma brick by brick

In my first business (the one selling cupcakes), things got *really* bad towards the end.

Did you ever play that game at kids' parties where you would put your forehead on a broomstick and spin round, then had to find your way to a chair across the room? Well, in case you missed out on that 80s' classic party game, obviously the idea was that you were completely dizzy and disoriented as you tried to find your way across the room to be the first to sit on the chair and win the packet of sweets.

Every single day of my life felt like that.

It was permanent disorientation, and I was piling problem on to problem as I moved so fast, telling myself if I could just get past this week then things would be easier, if I could just hit that revenue goal then everything would be ok ...

When it all came crashing down, I promised myself I would learn the lesson and never repeat the same mistakes, yet I found myself in a similar position (though certainly not as bad) ten years later when I was running my marketing agency. I couldn't see it as it was happening because it was cleverly disguised that time – everything looked and felt ok on the outside but on the inside (as in, inside me) I knew that things weren't right.

I was experienced enough to know that it's not ok to go home crying more evenings than not, to not sleep because your calendar is back to back the next day, or to get into the office at 6:30 am just so you can get some work done before the team come in and your brain is no longer able to function. I knew that it wasn't right, but I wasn't able to recognise why until I got my diagnosis.

If you have been through this process, I don't need to tell you – but for anyone who hasn't, it's like when you go for your eye test and you think you can see ok already but then they drop that one lens in front of your eyes and you're like, 'HOLY SHIT!! This is seeing?'

From that moment, everything changed. I had the words to explain what I was feeling and *why* I was feeling it – and that made such a difference. I could begin to recognise and work through the trauma I had experienced as a direct link to being neurodivergent:

- The difficulty I'd had maintaining friendships.
- The struggles I had experienced with my finances as a result of impulsive spending.
- The way I had used alcohol and recreational drugs to mask social anxiety and boost dopamine.
- All the ways that distress at failure, criticism or rejection, perceived or actual, had threaded through my life and impacted every single area of it.

There is a saying in the ADHD community: 'it's an explanation, not an excuse.' When I received my diagnosis, I was able to give myself some of the compassion I so freely gave others, and so I allowed myself to remove some of the shame and guilt I carried for the things I could never quite understand in my life and give my inner child some of the answers that she so desperately still needed.

I don't want to give the impression that this was an overnight thing – the grief/relief cycle continued for a good six months, but during that time I feel like everything changed for me.

I no longer found myself saying I had a migraine or an appointment so I could leave the office because I was completely overwhelmed and experiencing sensory overload. I would just go.

I no longer pretended to listen when someone talked me through a spreadsheet that they had taken time to put together but I was unable to focus on. I would ask them to send it to me so I could process it in my own time.

I no longer struggled through meetings with rage building inside because it was badly run or there wasn't a clear objective. I would ask for an agenda and say I could stay for 15 minutes.

My diagnosis made me better at business generally, but worse at that business in particular.

I could no longer ignore the things about business that had kept me in a destructive cycle for 13 years at that point, not just a burnout cycle but one of:

- self-abandonment to the point of making myself ill
- absolute obsession to the point of putting everything else on hold
- a boom-and-bust cycle with money that paralleled the boom and bust in my energy cycles.

It was at this point that I started to understand what a better, Brain First future would look like.

Your Brain First business: Trauma and the Brain First business

Let's have a quick look at how trauma could be showing up in your business today – this is a great way to realise the day-to-day impact some of your childhood experiences have on you, even now.

No need to score these, but rather use them as reflection and validation points before we move on.

PATTERNS OF OVERWORKING AND PROVING

- Do you feel like you're only 'doing enough' when you're exhausted or overdelivering?
- Is resting hard for you unless it's been *earned* with productivity?
- Do you take on too many projects to avoid feeling like a failure or a fraud?
- Are you constantly reinventing your business because it never feels 'right' or 'ready'?

HYPER-INDEPENDENCE AND CONTROL

- Do you struggle to ask for help, even when you're overwhelmed?
- Do you avoid delegating because it feels safer to do everything yourself?
- Is it hard to trust that someone else will 'get it right' or not let you down?
- Do you keep your business small (or chaotic) because being visible or successful feels unsafe?

PEOPLE-PLEASING AND BOUNDARIES

- Do you undercharge, over-give or say yes when you want to say no?
- Do you avoid setting clear boundaries because you fear disappointing people?
- Do you find yourself shaping your offers or messaging to be 'acceptable' or 'safe' for others?
- Is conflict or negative feedback something you'll do anything to avoid, even at your own expense?

SHAME, SELF-DOUBT AND PERFECTIONISM

- Do you feel you're never doing enough, no matter how hard you work?
- Do you spiral when you make a mistake or miss a deadline?
- Is your self-worth tied to how much you achieve or how perfect things look?
- Do you avoid launching or showing up consistently because it doesn't feel good enough yet?

EXECUTIVE DYSFUNCTION AND EMOTIONAL TRIGGERS

- Do small admin tasks or decisions cause massive emotional resistance?
- Do you shut down or avoid work when you feel overwhelmed, even if the task is small?
- Do you procrastinate because the fear of failing, being judged or getting it wrong is paralysing?
- Do you sometimes question whether you're really 'cut out' for running a business at all?

How do you feel after reading through those? If you had more than a few penny-drop moments there, then I am really excited for you to read the rest of the book and get the permission you need to build the business you deserve.

Tackling this stuff isn't easy and won't be 'fixed' by reading this book, but knowledge is power and having the words to describe what is going on for you is often the gateway to self-acceptance and finally acknowledging that something needs to change for you.

Side note: this stuff can feel heavy and can even bring up thoughts and feelings that you weren't aware were bubbling away under the surface. If you need some time to reflect and process, go and do that in a way that feels safe as well as kind to yourself.

Reframing what you thought you knew

When thinking about trauma in relation to ADHD and how it impacts our business (and our lives), it's good to remember that if there is a pattern of behaviour that you find disruptive in your life, and you can now recognise it as a learnt behaviour that stems from trauma, you can unlearn it. It might not be easy, but understanding that it's not *who* you are, it's *what* you do, can be so powerful.

We aren't responsible for what happened to us in our childhood, but once we know, we are responsible for healing from it.

TL;DR

We need to recognise there is trauma attached to living with ADHD and understand how that impacts us if we are to build a Brain First business.

Trauma impacts our business in ways we probably aren't even able to recognise immediately.

It's good to know that any learnt behaviour can be unlearnt.

3

The brilliance of being you

Identifying our strengths and why we tend to focus on our weaknesses

"I have this saying which I use with clients 'champagne dreams, lemonade energy'. In other words, ADHD business owners tend to have the ideas, and the clarity on the vision to such an extent that we can feel it. But we have a Vision Gap, which is that when we come to make it happen, we fall short on the execution.

Understanding your strengths is the key to your success

A few years post-diagnosis I had a conversation with another entrepreneur and they pointed out that where I would once talk about failures in business with reason and logic – having a good overview of the situation and what factors were at play – I now put it all down to ADHD and so bore the full weight of responsibility.

It was a real moment of insight for me as I realised that as helpful as connecting the dots of our past is, when we finally have this information about our brain, it can easily become the *only* lens we view ourselves through – and it's all too common for that lens to focus on the negative.

Living with a brain that needs to understand everything with a granular degree of certainty, and – through trauma response or learnt behaviour – is quick to blame itself for anything that it doesn't get that certainty on, can lead to a default negativity bias.

Putting all of this together, ADHD brains will, by default, try to get to the bottom of every problem. And because we've been trained to think we're at fault (remember that stat about neurodivergent kids hearing negative comments about themselves so much more frequently than other children, which is the root of our ADHD negativity lens?), unless we have definitive proof otherwise, we'll assume the issue lies with us, and with ADHD specifically.

- We dwell on the bad comment in a sea of lovely ones.
- We focus on the side eye from a stranger that we'll never see again.
- We remember the times we mess up more than we succeed.

And so in business, the big and small wins go to some hard drive never to be looked at again (sound familiar?) while the failures stay in full view on the desktop with no option to delete or minimise.

And it's the same with our strengths and weaknesses. We are so much more familiar with our perceived weaknesses than we are with our incredible strengths. If I asked you to give me five of each, I can almost guarantee you would have no problem listing the weaknesses but would struggle to get past the first few strengths. (Go on, try it ... was I right?)

I will put my hands up and say I am guilty of using the word superpower when it comes to ADHD. I get why people don't like it, and I understand that to some it really doesn't feel that way, but I think it's important to acknowledge the areas in which it *can be a strength*, without applying toxic positivity. For example, in your personal life, hyperfocus could be an absolute nightmare because you forget to eat, drink or turn up to see your friends on time because you were laser focused on your third new hobby of the month, but in business it absolutely can be a superpower as you can finally tear through tasks that you have been putting off for weeks because the perfect conditions needed to kickstart hyperfocus have finally aligned.

And so it's really important that you can identify your unique strengths, especially in the awareness phase of building a Brain First business. Because the awareness phase is about understanding *all* the factors that contribute to building your business:

- *the* ADHD brain
- *your* ADHD brain
- not just your weaknesses but your unique strengths as well
- your vision and goals.

Only when we understand this can we begin to build a business that works for our brain, without compromising on our ambitions. You see, this isn't a zero-sum game; we don't have to choose between our brain and our bank balance – if we can decondition ourselves from the 'rules' of business, and realise that those rules were never meant for us, then we can allow ourselves to create something incredible.

And when you consider that at the heart of this is our unique brain, unique strengths and unique vision, doesn't it kind of make sense that we need a unique business for them to live in?

So, what's going on? The ADHD connection

I have this saying which I use with clients: 'champagne dreams, lemonade energy'. In other words, ADHD business owners tend to have the ideas and the clarity on the vision to such an extent that we can *feel* it. But we have a Vision Gap, which is that when we come to make it happen, we fall short on the execution.

In the beginning we just try to make it happen and cobble it together as we go along, but after a while, we begin to see the pattern and so lose trust in ourselves – the confident, energetic entrepreneur soon becomes cautious, self-doubting and stuck as the failed ideas and plans start piling up and instead of 'wow, that sounds amazing!', you start hearing 'here we go again ...' from those around you.

Or, if you don't hear it, you sense it, which can often feel worse.

But what about, instead of blaming ourselves and seeing this as a personal flaw, we understand what is really going on.

In Chapter 1 I told you the prefrontal cortex was one of the four areas that is impaired in an ADHD brain, and this area is responsible for executive function, i.e. the 'what do I need to do next?' bit.

Understanding that shifts the blame from you as a person and removes the need to feel any sense of shame or failure, because it's just the way your brain works. The key here is understanding it, accepting it and planning for it.

Let's look at this objectively. You're on an episode of *The Apprentice* TV show and it's one of those food tasks where you are making cookies to sell on the street. The task needs:

- a project manager
- someone to create the product
- someone to sell on the street
- someone to manage the budget
- someone to get the product from the kitchen to the team on the street.

In this scenario, it's really easy for us to say, 'I would be good at this role but not at this one' – right? And more than that, we know that if we are put in charge of, for example, creating the product, we would absolutely SMASH it because we have experience in that area, or we are really creative, or we have a great eye. But if we are put in charge of, for example, the budget, the whole team are likely to fail the task because we don't have the best sense for numbers or detail. It's so obvious.

And yet, when it comes to our business, the thing responsible for our income, putting food on our table and our holidays, we are prepared to take that risk because we think we should be able to do it all ourselves (and let's face it, in the early days, we have to!) and asking for help feels deeply uncomfortable.

Listen, Richard Branson once stopped a board meeting to ask his accountant to explain the difference between gross and net profit! It's ok to ask for help.[12]

In this awareness-raising phase of building a Brain First business, the goal is to reach a point of acceptance, a place where you don't need to do mental gymnastics telling yourself that you 'should' be able to do XYZ because other people can. It's irrelevant what anyone else can (or can't) do, all that matters is understanding what *your* unique strengths are and, *second* to that, your weaknesses.

Because once you know, and accept your weaknesses, you can focus on your strengths and build your business with joy, confidence and conviction.

My Brain First journey: The second business

After I sold my second business, the marketing agency, I was lucky enough to be able to take some time to recalibrate. I think we have this idea that once we remove the thing that was causing us to burn out or was frazzling our nervous system, we're suddenly ok, but it really doesn't happen that way.

There was definitely the immediate relief of not having to be 'on call' and releasing the pressure of responsibility, but in terms of rebalancing my nervous system – there was work to do.

In the immediate aftermath, I told myself I was never again going to build a business that needed a team. The understanding I had gained about how I worked best led me to believe, at that time, that working alone was the best thing for me. Communication can be exhausting for ADHDers and the phrase 'go fast alone, go far together' just never really felt like something that applied to me. But in the few years since, I have realised that the key for me is actually working with the *right* people, in the *right* way – so I don't have a team as such, but I work with absolute experts in their fields whom I can pull in when I need them. I have a wonderful assistant who I couldn't live without, I have a brilliant tech guy who is on hand when I wave the flag, and accountants and solicitors who I have worked with for more than ten years. This works really well for me. That isn't to say the same will be true for you, but I do know a huge number of ADHD/ND business owners feel the same way.

Thinking about how to create my own truly Brain First business led me to the understanding that I wanted to make maximum impact with *manageable* effort. You'll notice I don't say minimum effort, because that wasn't the goal. I LOVE working (my therapist would tell you this is a high achiever/avoidant trauma response, but let's bypass that for now), so the goal was never to *not* work but rather to work on the things that make me feel capable, rewarded and energised. For me, this looked like supporting other ADHD business owners and founders to understand their own brain better and shape their business around it – which is where I am now. I love the work I do, whether it's one-to-one client work, consultancy or sharing content. I am so proud to be a voice in the ADHD business community that is supporting founders to realise their dreams (perhaps by realising their dreams aren't quite what they thought they were!).

Your Brain First business: Understanding your strengths

Let's pause here to get a good understanding of your personal strengths. It's easy to assume that you know them, but you might be surprised when you actually go through them one by one.

Using this list of key business strengths, let's plot your profile on the radar chart below. To do this, score each area (communication, leadership, marketing, etc) out of 5. An area that you consider a strength would get a low mark, and an area that you consider a weakness (or one to develop) would score higher.

In each segment, put an X in the space that relates to the score you've chosen. At the end you can connect the Xs from segment to segment to give your ADHD a visual shape. When you look at the results:

- Were they what you were expecting or does anything surprise you?
- Are you consistent across all areas or do you 'spike' in one (indicating a particular strength or weakness)?

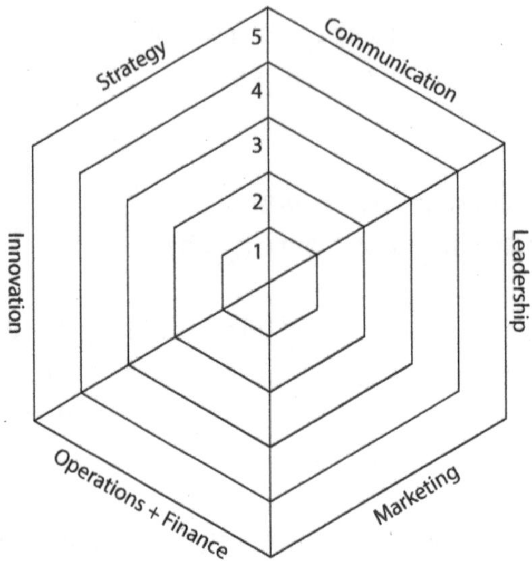

This isn't a scientific assessment, so don't worry about getting a question 'wrong', but it will give you a quick visual aid of where your strengths lie so that you have a clear understanding as you go through the book. It also isn't about how 'good' or 'bad' at business you are, so try to approach it objectively – you will notice that not all the areas are relevant to your business anyway.

STRATEGY

- Vision clarity – Has a clear direction and long-term goals
- Decision-making – Makes confident, timely and data-informed decisions
- Market awareness – Understands the competitive landscape and shifting trends
- Business model design – Can craft a sustainable and scalable model
- Problem-solving – Handles setbacks and challenges proactively

COMMUNICATION

- Storytelling – Captivates and connects with audiences through narrative
- Negotiation – Navigates deals and partnerships effectively
- Public speaking – Communicates clearly and confidently in front of others
- Copywriting – Writes persuasive content that sells or educates
- Feedback delivery – Gives and receives constructive input with maturity

LEADERSHIP

- Team building – Attracts and develops the right people
- Delegation – Assigns responsibility without micromanaging
- Conflict resolution – Addresses tension with fairness and clarity
- Coaching/mentoring – Helps others grow within the business
- Accountability culture – Sets expectations and follows through

MARKETING

- Customer insight – Has a deep understanding of who the ideal customer is
- Brand positioning – Creates a clear, compelling place in the market
- Lead generation – Knows how to attract consistent interest
- Sales conversion – Turns leads into paying customers
- Retention and loyalty – Builds long-term customer relationships

OPERATIONAL AND FINANCIAL

- Process development – Creates efficient systems and standard operating procedures (SOPs)
- Project management – Keeps timelines and teams aligned
- Financial literacy – Understands cash flow, profit, pricing, margins
- Resource allocation – Invests time, money and energy wisely
- Risk management – Plans for uncertainty and protects the business

INNOVATION AND GROWTH STRENGTHS

- Product development – Creates offers people truly want
- Adaptability – Adjusts quickly to change or feedback
- Continuous learning – Stays curious and keeps improving
- Tech-savviness – Embraces tools that boost productivity or reach
- Partnership building – Leverages networks and collaborations

What have you found? Remember that building a Brain First business is all about figuring out the things you're good at – not about focusing on the areas you think need development. Remember what we said earlier about the negativity bias? It's time to be radical and let that go. If there's an area you find challenging, you should feel empowered to handle it differently or delegate it to someone for whom it's a natural fit – without any guilt. The most important thing with this exercise is to recognise and really internalise your *strengths*. These are the things that make you the brilliant entrepreneur you are, so celebrate and lean into them.

Reframing what you thought you knew

Maybe you're reading this book because you are at the point where you simply cannot carry on running your business the way you currently are, or perhaps you are ok with how you run it but would like to make a few improvements. Whichever one you are, know that it's not *nothing* to take an idea and turn it into a business that generates money and supports your livelihood.

It's not *nothing* to turn your back on a stable, reliable income with benefits and progression to pursue your dream.

It's not *nothing* to ride the rollercoaster every day, regardless of how scary it is, getting back up and strapping yourself in to go again.

We are alchemists, we turn our dreams into reality, our ideas into money – and just starting the whole enterprise is a strength in itself.

TL;DR

To build your custom-fit Brain First business, you must know your strengths ... and lean into them.

4

Radical acceptance

Starting out small

> "A common misconception with people I work with is that the goal is to 'fix' aspects of their ADHD that feel most challenging to them. And while the purpose is always to lessen the impact of those traits, so that life and business feel easier, coming from a place of needing 'fixing' is really the wrong way to view it.

As we discussed in the last chapter, building your Brain First business is about understanding yourself and your specific strengths and leaning into them. And as I mentioned in the Introduction, it is also about opening your eyes to the fact that the business world is stacked against you, recognising that traditional business standards are neurotypical standards, and accepting that there is another way that can set you free, put you back in charge and allow you to achieve any goal that you truly want.

The Brain First concept is rooted in radical acceptance. Unless you truly and deeply accept yourself and the way your brain works, you will forever be battling against it and bullying yourself into being 'better' at life. To be fixed, something has to be broken, and nothing about you is broken apart from the expectations you are allowing the world to place on you and the systems you think you have to use to meet them.

Now, I imagine you might be using that 'all or nothing' thinking that we are blessed with to see acceptance as a perfect utopia where we dance around in floaty dresses and open-necked shirts, living in perfect harmony and only stopping to say good morning to the fairies and baby animals that pass us by. But this is no Disney movie, this is real life, and I don't know about you but I am as far from perfect as it gets, so this is not how acceptance looks to me. My version of acceptance looks like:

- not beating myself up if I am struggling to do a 'simple' task or follow through on an idea
- not making up an excuse to get out of an engagement if I don't have the mental or energetic capacity, but being honest about why I need the down time
- taking time to consider opportunities before shouting YES because the dopamine is dripping in my brain, then regretting it the moment I realise the practical implication of yet another project
- listening to my body and brain and prioritising what they need over what I want (most of the time).

Does that mean I *never* do those things? Absolutely not! In fact, I'll let you into a secret: I sometimes feel like a total fraud because I'm preaching about being Brain First while I am balancing an overbooked week with a toddler who isn't sleeping, perimenopause symptoms and a bottleneck of work that I'm drowning under. But does that mean I haven't built a Brain First business? No, it means I am a human with ADHD and life doesn't always go to plan.

In those moments, acceptance is my saviour and it reminds me of what I can – and can't – control.

It reminds me that everything is temporary and that if I cancel a call or push back a deadline, the world won't end.

So, what's going on? The ADHD connection

After years of absorbing negative messages and broken promises (to ourselves and others), many people with ADHD have a fragile relationship with self-trust. So, when we are told there is a way to do something, we will try to do it exactly like that, and if we aren't able to do it the accepted way, we see it as a personal failure.

How many times have you been nervous to talk about your business because you don't do it the way you 'should'? You might have had a meeting with a bank manager or a mentor or even just a mate in the pub and felt that pang of 'please don't ask me about (insert your personal nemesis here)' as the topic of your business comes up.

Do you have a set process that you follow religiously? I'm willing to bet the answer is no. Could you tell anyone your forecasted cashflow for the next 12 months? I'm guessing that's a no, too.

You feel like a fraud, even though your way works.

The most common misconception I hear from ADHD business owners is that they think the goal is to 'cure' their ADHD to a point where they can run their business in a neurotypical way.

I'm willing to bet that your first year as an entrepreneur will have followed a path similar to this:

- Great! I've got a business!
- Great! I'm making money!
- Wow! This feels so easy, why doesn't everyone do it?
- Sorry – I have to pay how much in taxes?
- Oh, I have to tell you how much I owe? How do I know?
- I should have filed *what* form?
- And now I have to pay that fine? Great ...

I know it's a stereotype, but it is for a reason. Getting started is easy – keeping going, not so much.

This is just one of the ways that our century-old, neurotypical-focused business model doesn't work for our brain. Now obviously I am not going to be able to eradicate taxes, or magically make you like filling out forms, but I am going to help you see that those things that we perceive as weaknesses are entirely manageable and should never be the reason we don't succeed in business (or the reason we don't start in the first place).

Imagine speaking to an artist. They are talking about a piece they're working on, describing the colours and story behind the piece, totally lost in the emotions it stirs up in them. They look for a reaction and someone says, 'That sounds great. Can you create a spreadsheet with a detailed breakdown of the time it will take and the paints you will use?'

You need to be the artist, not the spreadsheet-for-no-purpose guy. Don't apply 'business' logic to a situation it doesn't need to be applied to just because you think there's a way things 'should' be done.

How many times have you created a business plan, marketing strategy or any other document you thought you ought to have, only to find it years later in your drive and realise you never looked at it again? Whether you are an artist or a lawyer or a baker or a consultant, there is a way of applying Brain First logic to your business and banishing the 'just because' ways, for ever.

My goal for anyone building a Brain First business is to forget all the business standards we so readily accept and reimagine what business looks like for *you*. When you were young and naive, before you understood the realities of running a business, what did you dare to dream it might look like?

That is the goal.

Claire's Brain First journey: Recalibrating your business standards

Let me tell you a quick story about a client – we'll call her Claire. Claire came to me ready to throw in the towel. She had been working on her 'dream' for three years and although she'd had some pockets of success, she just couldn't maintain the energy needed to be 'always on' and drive the revenue to hit her goals.

Our original conversation went something like this:

> Me: Ok, so what is the goal?
>
> Claire: £20k per month
>
> Me: Ok, cool – why £20k?
>
> Claire: Because I'm stuck at £17k, so I want to get to £20k.
>
> Me: And what would £20k mean for you?
>
> Claire: What do you mean?
>
> Me: Well, for example, you told me you wanted more time with your younger children. Will hitting £20k help you do that?
>
> Claire: Mmmm, maybe, but I'd have to spend more time working to begin with, I guess.
>
> Me: Ok, so would you be able to hit £20k with the same resources you have now?
>
> Claire: I'd probably need one more person to support me.
>
> Me: And what would that cost?
>
> Claire: About £3k?
>
> Me: Ok, so you're back to £17k, which is what you did this month?
>
> Claire: Oh. Yeah.
>
> Me: Can I just ask what is 'enough' for you? I don't mean just enough, I mean enough to live the life you want to live, go on holiday, spend time with the kids and be able to buy overpriced skincare without feeling sick?
>
> Claire: Well, I can do all that now and spend time with my family ...

I could see the realisation sweep over her as the colour came back into her face. She – like so many of us – was working to the dream we've been sold on Instagram or in a podcast that business is only about growth, or getting awards or building teams, or exiting, and yes, that is what some people's businesses look like – but if yours doesn't look like that, then that's ok, too. It's still a business.

Whenever I think of Claire, I am reminded of the parable of the Brazilian fisherman. A wealthy businessman meets a fisherman in a small Brazilian village and asks why he isn't working longer hours to grow his fishing business. The fisherman explains he catches enough to support his family and then spends the rest of his day relaxing, playing music, spending time with friends and enjoying life.

The businessman suggests a long-term plan: fish more, buy a bigger boat, start a company and eventually retire rich. The fisherman asks what he'd do after retiring. The businessman replies, 'Then you could relax, fish a little, play music and enjoy time with friends' – exactly what the fisherman was already doing.

Moral of the story: sometimes we already have the life we're striving for, and more success doesn't always mean more happiness.

Your Brain First business: Starting small

So how do we pare back the neurotypical layers to do things our way? The key is to start small. This isn't about throwing the baby out with the bathwater or doing our usual trick of changing everything overnight, then getting completely overwhelmed and changing precisely nothing – like all those times you had a sudden urge to Marie Kondo your wardrobe, then looked at the pile of clothes all over your bed and wished you had never started. No, this is about getting really honest with yourself and being prepared to challenge your own ideas of success.

Let's stay with that for a moment: what is your idea of success?

When I ask most people, like Claire, they will tell me a financial goal, perhaps a monthly revenue or even personal income target, but when I start questioning them on it, they can rarely tell me why.

So many of our ideas of success are ideals absorbed from the content we consume: from social media to podcasts, to the press and TV, we see the lifestyle and hear the chat from 'experts', and somehow their goal of a 10k/100k/10 million month becomes ours, too.

Rarely do we stop to question:

- Are they actually achieving that? (Almost definitely not.)
- Do I even *really* want it?

Because while the idea of the positive impact of money coming in is vivid in your mind and sold to us by society, we can fail to think through whether that's the goal we should really aim for, whether it's right for us, exactly *how* we might achieve it and (more importantly) at what cost.

It's one of the many ways we are setting ourselves up to fail. We are setting goals that aren't ours, which require skills we don't have and need us to work in a way that doesn't suit us.

Here is a way of goal setting that I love to use with clients, and I think you will love too.

BRAIN FIRST GOAL SETTING

Instead of just the *outcome* you desire, you also name:

- why it matters (aligning with your values)
- how it feels (create an emotional anchor)
- what success looks like *for your brain*.

Bonus question: *What would make this easier for my brain?*

Example:

- Goal: Create a digital product for my audience.
- Why: I want more income without burning out from one-to-one interactions.
- Feels like: Calm, in control, proud.
- Brain-First success:
  - no burnout
  - broken into microtasks
  - built during high-energy hours.

What would make this easier for my brain? For example, getting design and marketing support to launch the product.

Change is hard, but making the changes needed to become Brain First is the only way to achieve sustainable success. And remember that you can use and repeat this process for both big goals (like starting a business) and small goals (such as filing taxes on time).

Reframing what you thought you knew

If you can go back to basics and revisit what success *truly* looks like to you – not your friends or peers – then you can build a business that allows you to put yourself at the centre of it and work to your true strengths and achieve your real goals, rather than staying in the miserable cycle of aiming for the moon and landing in burnout.

TL;DR

Set goals that align with what you really want to achieve (not what society tells you) and establish ways of reaching them that are based on your own ways of working – not those from a textbook.

Change is a conscious decision, but you can stack the baby steps to create big shifts.

Radical acceptance of your strengths and needs will help you set goals and take steps that get you where you want to be, without blame and burnout. This is the work of alignment: making sure your business is working for your brain and building on your strengths. We're coming on to this in the next Part.

PART II

Alignment

Your Brain First business

Your guide to Part II

All too often for ADHD entrepreneurs, what started off as *exciting, so much fun* and *such an adventure* quickly turns into overwhelm, burnout and perhaps even dread at the thought of another day chasing your tail and looking like you've 'got this'.

As the responsibilities pile up, so do the demands, emails and need to be 'always on'. So that spark of an idea you ran with and made into an actual business, with actual customers, making actual money, went from being your greatest source of pride to a cage that you feel trapped inside. Except you're not quite ready to admit that to anyone, so the mask stays firmly in place and whenever people ask, 'How's business going?', you reply, 'Yeah, great thanks.'

And you're not lying either – perhaps it is going great from a 'business' perspective: you're busy, your clients/customers are happy and you're making money, which, in some ways, is what makes this scenario even more painful. We begin to tell ourselves:

- Everyone else can handle the pressure – why am I so useless?
- All I have to do is follow the plan, why can't I even do that?
- Maybe if I had a new system, then I would feel more in control and everything would be ok?

The internal struggle becomes more and more shame-filled as we look around us and see others handling situations that are leaving us overwhelmed and burnt out. But there is something hard about admitting to feeling like this. It's not just saying it out loud, it's because it raises the question: 'Well, now what?' You're so deep in and you don't want to quit – you just don't want to feel like you are pretending any more.

And that, my friend, is at the very heart of why we ADHD entrepreneurs need to find alignment between ourselves and our businesses so that we don't feel this disconnect between our internal and external worlds.

And I know you'll know exactly what I mean by that.

This section is all about identifying the areas of our businesses where we actually need to make the changes. This isn't about cracking a walnut with a sledge hammer, but rather about gaining an understanding about the areas we are currently fighting against each day, that could be so much easier to navigate.

This is often the step we miss: we gain the understanding and then jump in to make the changes, but without really assessing what changes we need to make. This is where overwhelm comes in, because I can almost guarantee you don't need to change *everything* about your business – you just need to understand the areas that are causing you most brain-pain so that we can fix them, together.

As you go through the chapters, push yourself to explore the areas of your business that feel most challenging and use the chapter exercises to go even deeper. Go through each exercise as you read the chapter. Doing this will help you build your 'Brain First Toolkit'. Remember that you can also find these exercises online at http://book.brainfirst.co.

Take your time going through this section. Remember that this isn't a race. Some of these chapters will challenge you, and that's a good thing. Just keep in mind always your goal of building your Brain First business and apply some rebellious self-trust – you know your business better than anyone.

5 The business of business

When did it get so complicated?

> Our brain will do anything to get dopamine, so if it can see a little dopamine-shaped treat in creating a solution to a problem that doesn't exist, it will convince you that it's time well spent.

Business is actually really simple: 'an organisation that provides goods and services to the community in exchange for money, with the goal of becoming profitable'.[13]

Straightforward, right?

But in the same way that a new parent can simplify their job to 'just keeping the baby alive', it's in the long list of tasks that go into that mission that the complication and exhaustion happen.

For a business owner, it's easy to simplify our role into bullet points such as:

- Create the product
- Sell the product
- Operate the business to maximise profitability

In reality this looks more like:

- Create the product
  - Perform market research
  - Design the product
  - Test the product
  - Re-iterate if necessary
  - Price the product
- Sell the product
  - Create a marketing plan for the product
  - Allocate a budget to the marketing plan
  - Learn the skills or hire the experts to execute the plan
  - Test the plan
  - Optimise the plan
  - Analyse the results
  - Be aware of new trends and platform updates to incorporate into the plan
- Operate the business in a way that maximises profitability
  - Account for every penny coming in and going out of the business
  - Perform regular analysis of business costs
  - Negotiate with suppliers to maintain best rates
  - Forecast revenue across the quarter and year
  - Report against those figures
  - Adjust forecast where necessary

- Create P+L report
- Complete annual tax assessments.

And, as you will know, within each of those sub-tasks there are a million micro-tasks to consider. Business always has the potential to be complicated, but the ADHD brain makes it that bit harder as we tend to ramp up the difficulty by adding in *more* jobs rather than paring things back.

This is where business gets messy.

We over-complicate it because:

- we think that we have to: we see others doing it and think that's the way it should be done
- we thrive in chaos: the truth is, our brain craves the dopamine we get from chaos and we quickly become comfortable working that way.

Basically, we get lost. We take a few wrong turns and before we know it ... we're driving in completely the wrong direction with no sense of a final destination.

Have you heard of the Pareto Principle? It's a theory applied to business by Joseph M Juran in 1941 after he read the works of the Italian economist Vilfredo Pareto, who had observed that 80 per cent of the land in Italy was owned by 20 per cent of the people.[14]

Juran loved this insight and applied it to his business clients, initially in the field of quality control. These days it is used across just about every measure in business. The principle states that roughly 80 per cent of outcome comes from 20 per cent of input. In business, this could mean:

- 80 per cent of profits come from 20 per cent of customers.
- 80 per cent of sales come from 20 per cent of products.
- 80 per cent of results come from 20 per cent of effort.

It's the last one that I like to focus on when building a Brain First business, because to an ADHD brain that experiences the daily fight for focus and energy, the realisation that 80 per cent of the work we do isn't contributing to our success, is – quite frankly – sickening.

So, what's going on? The ADHD connection

A blessing and a curse of ADHD is that we are natural problem solvers. We go through life like solution-seeking missiles and can often spot a problem from a million miles away. This is a highly valuable skill to have in business, but can also be the reason we over-complicate things. Our brain will do anything to get dopamine. Remember the chapter opening observation that if it can see a little dopamine-shaped treat in creating a solution to a problem that doesn't exist, it will convince you that it's time well spent? This means that rather than sticking to our day-to-day business, we'll easily get distracted with problems that aren't really problems and waste time creating solutions that don't move our business forward.

If we want to keep our businesses simple in structure and focus on the 20 per cent of effort that gives us 80 per cent of the rewards, then we do need to be radically honest with ourselves.

This sounds simple but it means you gotta do The Work on yourself – and The Work isn't always easy ... or fun! The Work for you might be using therapy to address low self-esteem that is impacting your business, or it might mean cleaning up your reliance on cheap dopamine (i.e. stop reaching for your phone as an avoidance tactic, or chasing the shiny new thing instead of dealing with the boring old thing that needs addressing).

Roei's Brain First business

Roei Samuel is the founder and CEO of Connectd, a platform that connects start-ups with investors. The company saw phenomenal growth over its first five years in business, going from $135,000 ARR (annual recurring revenue) with a team of 5 in 2020 to $14.2 million with a team of 105 in 2025.

Roei was diagnosed with ADHD and dyslexia at a young age. When he reflects on his career he can see times when he lost focus on his core business model, and also times when he lost focus on himself.

Before Roei started Connectd, he cut his teeth creating RealSport, a content platform for sports and gaming fans to build podcasts, blogs and videos. At a time when everyone had a blog but no one had an audience, RealSport delivered a recommendation engine that cross-pollinated content, resulting in a thriving ecosystem of creators.

Despite having no formal business training, Roei's hyperfocus, creativity and appetite for jumping and learning how to fly on the way down drove RealSport to 9 million monthly users. It landed partnerships with the Premier League, the NBA and the NFL. In 2018, at just 26, Roei sold the company to gaming giant Gfinity – a life-changing acquisition that took him from deep credit card debt to self-made millionaire overnight.

But that's not the full story.

The ADHD traits that powered RealSport's growth also nearly derailed it. In 2016, Roei pursued a high-stakes opportunity to launch a Premier League FIFA tournament without proper licensing in place. It was impulsive, thrilling – and almost fatal for the business. Platform usage dropped 50 per cent as the team neglected day-to-day operations.

Looking back at this point, Roei can see that his ADHD craving for the dopamine hit nearly cost him his company. 'We nearly lost everything because I got obsessed with the shiny new thing,' he says. 'The whole company depended on my involvement, so if I was distracted ... the whole business suffered.'

Later, at Connectd, Roei found the same patterns reappearing. With the company in a rapid expansion phase, Roei gained over 40 kg (almost 90 lbs) in weight and was stuck in a cycle of toxic dopamine hits and burnout.

'I realised: I will not be a good CEO unless I change how I manage my ADHD. I had fallen into the trap so many of us do: deep hyperfocus, late nights, never leaving my desk, eating and drinking crap and living dopamine hit to dopamine hit.'

That year, he overhauled everything. Diet. Sleep. Exercise. Boundaries. He replaced chaos with structure – not rigidly, but intentionally. ADHD management became a non-negotiable part of his leadership. He shifted from adrenaline-fuelled sprints to sustainable momentum.

And importantly, Roei started to delegate. So rather than spending 80 per cent of his time on tasks that didn't need him directly, he could concentrate on the 20 per cent that would bring in the results. 'I spend a month shadowing every senior hire. Once they are up to speed, I let them run. I back them like founders – if it fails, we learn. If it flies, amazing.'

Roei gave key team members generous equity and built a culture where everyone feels like an owner. This model of high-trust leadership helped him step out of the day-to-day and build a scalable, founder-light structure, which he knew was his version of a Brain First business.

Roei admits that learning to delegate was one of his hardest lessons. 'At RealSport, I couldn't let go. I needed to know everything. At Connectd, I trust my team. I still have seven or eight direct reports, but now they feed back to me – I don't run everything.'

He recognises this isn't something you can do from day one – you have to hit a certain revenue and head count to build the team that allows you to relinquish some of that control. He views his team as entrepreneurs within the business. Some stay, others move on when their 'project' ends. That fluid, pitch-led culture keeps Connectd innovative, agile and, most importantly, aligned with the way Roei works best.

Roei's journey is a blueprint for building a business around your brain. His dopamine-craving ADHD brain gave him vision, momentum and a fearless approach to risk – but also nearly cost him everything when unmanaged. The second time around, he paired impulsivity with insight. He built infrastructure around his strengths, empowered a high-trust team and shifted from burnout to balance.

Roei understands his 80:20 and built his whole business around it – the results speak for themselves.

This isn't a story of masking ADHD to succeed. It's a story of working *with* it – and building a multi-million-pound company in the process.

Your Brain First business: Mapping out your 80:20 vision

Now let's move on to ways you can start to understand your own 80:20.

1. REVIEWING HOW YOU SPEND YOUR TIME

First of all, we're going to do a quick exercise to help you identify where your strengths and personal interests lie (in other words, the parts of your business that will give you energy and keep you motivated), as well as figure out what is leaving you drained. We'll then move on to look at whether those tricky tasks should really be demanding your time.

There's no better place to unpick what's happening in your day-to-day working life than your calendar, so let's start with a random week in your diary. Try to choose one that is busy with a good mix of things going on. Now ask yourself:

- Which day looks the most fun? Can you identify why?
  - Is it quieter than the other days?
  - Does it have more creative tasks/meetings/social events than the other days?
  - Is it a day when you are working *in* your business or *on* your business?
- Which day fills you with dread already? Can you identify why?
  - Did you agree to an event that you know you don't want to go to?
  - Is the day full of the kind of work you least enjoy?
  - Is it too busy or too quiet?

2. ESTABLISHING YOUR VALUE/SKILL MATRIX

Now, let's use that information to understand whether the tasks you're doing are the best use of your time. Using the template below, try mapping out the tasks you personally do in the business and where they sit in the matrix. High and low skill refer to how easily the skill comes to you and how much you enjoy it; high and low value refer to how much it really contributes to your business success.

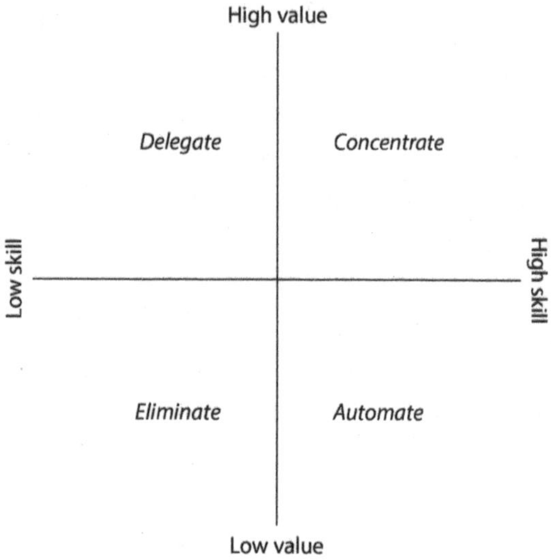

Once you have your results, this is what you will do:

Bottom Left (low skill/low value):
Eliminate: get rid of it! You don't need to do these things for your business to succeed.
Example: Spending an hour a week on creating a plan for TikTok content that you rarely get to execute because you just don't have the bandwidth isn't a good use of your time right now. Get rid.
Bottom Right (high skill/low value):
Automate: use a system to replace you doing the work. You may need to set up the system, but beyond that (and the odd check-in) you should not need to be involved.
Example: Rather than onboarding each client manually, set up your customer relationship management (CRM) system to email them their onboarding form, contract and first invoice.
Top Left (low skill/high value):

Delegate: pass these tasks on ASAP!
Example: Find a VA (virtual assistant) to manage your inbox so you are only left with the messages that you need to have input on.
Top Right (high skill/high value):
Concentrate: This is your zone – focus on the tasks in this area. This includes anything that requires your eyes, ears, face or voice.
Example: signing off important decisions or creating personal brand content.

3. ACTIONING YOUR 80:20 VISION

So, how do you plot this out in practice? It's time to start thinking about how your Brain First day and week, protecting the 20 per cent activities for the 80 per cent rewards, would look in reality. Doing this will help you understand the changes you need to make and where you need to start putting some boundaries in place (which also may mean getting comfortable with saying 'no').

Try creating your Brain First calendar in two stages:

1. Do it without overthinking it. What does your dream Brain First week look like – without considering which tasks you *have* to do?
2. Now plan your work while referencing your 80:20 matrix so you know which tasks you need to keep *for now* and which you can eliminate or delegate straight away.

Next, create a Brain First day using the template below:

My Brain First Day

TIME	ACTIVITY	BF SCORE

Complete this grid, keeping in mind the following questions/actions:

- What time would your ideal day begin?
- How would it start? I doubt it's by rolling out of bed and opening your laptop, so start with the things that set you up to do your best work, i.e. a walk, stretches, time with the kids.
- Then set the activity or activities for the day. Remember, the point of this isn't to only list 'reply to emails/do admin/call accountant'. Add in space for reflection, creativity and active relaxation.
- Finally, give it a Brain First score – mark the activity out of 10 as a rough measurement to track. If it's not something that's a '20 per cent' priority task, give it a low score (and try to delegate, automate or eliminate straight away). If it's something that's high value/high skill, give it a high score. Repeat the exercise again in six months so you can see the areas in which you have developed or changed.

Reframing what you thought you knew

Ultimately, there will be a list of things you have to do in your business – they are things that need your eyes, ears, face or voice. Everything else you should be working towards outsourcing or delegating.

Understanding your own 20 per cent of effort that achieves 80 per cent of results is absolutely key to achieving your Brain First business.

Remember, the goal isn't 'who can get the most done' but 'who can identify the right things to spend their time on, so they can keep going the longest'.

Remember: you can't build from burnout!

TL;DR

You're over-complicating business – stop that.

Keep in mind the Pareto Principle: 80 per cent of your outcomes come from 20 per cent of your effort. So when you need to make change (for yourself or for your business), take a look at your own 80:20 setup and refocus on the work that's having the biggest impact.

6

Goal setting

How to create goals that your brain cares about

> **Goal setting (and getting) looks starkly different for neurotypical and neurodivergent brains because our brains are wired to be motivated by very different-looking carrots.**

We all know that to be able to arrive at your destination, you need to know where (or what) it is. Like driving without an address in the sat nav, if we don't have business goals and targets, how will we know if we reach them?

But goal setting can be a tricky thing when you have a brain that is as unpredictable as a toddler – that one day can respond to goals with motivation and excitement, and the next with demand avoidance and, well, a tantrum.

Of course, this isn't about getting rid of goals entirely. If you have a team and overheads, then financial targets especially are unavoidable, but you can still analyse how you respond to them and what you are motivated and demotivated by, and recognise that what works for you may be very different from what works for those around you.

This is another time when being radically honest with yourself will pay dividends. By understanding yourself and your needs, you can start setting goals that are meaningful and achievable.

When you think about how you respond to goals:

- Do you generally find that you're motivated by them?
- Does it matter how they are set/presented or who sets them?
- Are you motivated by reward or overwhelmed by it?

All these questions are really important and we'll explore how to use self-reflection like this to set goals effectively in your business as we go through the chapter. But for now, take notice of your immediate response. For example, if your gut reaction to 'Are you motivated by reward?' is a loud and clear HELL NO, then try to dig a little deeper into that. What does reward mean to you? Does it make you feel a sense of pressure or does it instantly turn a goal into a demand for you?

A lot of the issues we experience around goal setting are the result of the external pressure we feel and the way it can trigger our demand avoidance, so understanding that can help you to understand that you need full autonomy when it comes to your goals. Personally, I know that while goals help with my vision planning, my demand avoidance can easily be triggered if I am working to *someone else's* goals in a project. I do best when I have a goal that I've set for myself – then just watch me go!

So, what's going on? The ADHD connection

Neurodivergent brains are motivated by very different goals from those of neurotypical brains, which means we need to think about things differently. If you're late diagnosed, you have likely been trying to work in a neurotypical way your whole life, so what we need to do now is unpick how you've understood goal setting in the past and figure out what will actually motivate you in the future.

Let's take a look at some of the differences.

EXECUTIVE FUNCTION AND PLANNING

Neurotypicals (those whose behaviours and processes align with society's norms): often have more reliable executive function, so they can break a big goal into smaller steps, hold those steps in working memory and follow through over time.

Neurodivergents (those whose behaviours and processes are more idiosyncratic): struggle with executive dysfunction, so even knowing where to start, or what's urgent versus important, can feel impossible. This leads to either avoidance or impulsive over-committing.

TIME PERCEPTION AND MOTIVATION

NTs: can mentally project into the future and delay gratification more easily, so long-term goals feel real and motivating.

NDs (especially with ADHD): struggle with time blindness (when it's hard to accurately estimate the time it may take to do something) and temporal discounting (valuing immediate rewards over those that are delayed), making the future feel fuzzy or irrelevant. Things are either happening 'now' or effectively not at all (the 'not now'). They find it hard to stay motivated unless the goal is immediate, urgent or emotionally charged.

CONSISTENCY VS INTENSITY

NTs: can usually chip away at goals consistently, even when they're bored or tired, due to a more predictable supply of dopamine.

NDs: tend to work in spurts of hyperfocus and then crash, which means traditional 'small daily habits' don't always stick.

NEED FOR CLARITY

NTs: can usually tolerate some discomfort in ambiguity/lack of clarity around tasks, helping them to keep a sense of perspective and avoiding overwhelm.

NDs: can become overwhelmed if tasks don't have clear next steps (figuring out what to do in these cases presents an executive functioning challenge), even if the goal is something they want to achieve. The risk of overwhelm increases as tasks become more complicated, meaning there's likely to be ambiguity around what exactly needs to happen and when.

PERFECTIONISM

NTs: can usually handle some imperfection and doing things 'just well enough'.

NDs: often experience paralysis from perfectionism and their close cousins, imposter syndrome and rejection sensitive dysphoria (RSD). We have a whole chapter on RSD later in the book when we'll explore it in more detail, but a simple definition would describe RSD as an intense reaction to *perceived*, *actual* or even *anticipated* rejection, criticism or failure, triggering emotional (and physical) pain, shame or anger – often out of proportion to the situation. RSD links to perfectionism because the fear of coming across anything that could be interpreted as criticism (even if it's meant constructively) causes us to throw absolutely everything at a task, even to our own detriment. Imposter syndrome feeds into this as well, as the fear of being 'caught out' for not being good enough also causes us to spin the hamster wheel even harder.

INTERNAL VS EXTERNAL MOTIVATION

NTs: may feel naturally motivated by a sense of obligation or achievement.

NDs: unless driven by hyperfocus, often need a dopamine injection from a task being novel or involving an element of competition or urgency to kickstart action. If a goal feels emotionally disconnected or meaningless, they'll avoid it – even if it's important.

What does all of this mean?

It means understanding that the way you set goals and are motivated to achieve them, even if that's different from the way other people would handle them, isn't a character flaw or personality quirk, it's down to the way your brain is wired from birth. Accepting this is key to giving yourself permission to do things the Brain First way.

No more 'should's, no more checking what everyone else is doing first. This is about your unique vision and your unique way of achieving it.

My Brain First journey: Goals and motivation

I'm going to go a bit off-topic at this point and veer away from the business world, but I think this part of my life is pretty instructive for our purposes too.

In all honesty, I have had no bigger goal in life than having a baby. Like many of us, I grew up assuming my life would mirror my mum's. In my case that meant married by 17 and having my first baby at the ripe old age of 21.

I guess, on reflection, it's not that I thought it would happen *exactly* like that, but there was a gradually increasing sense of failure and mild panic every birthday after my 21st that I wasn't 'on track' to hit this predefined timeline.

I had a few 'serious' relationships (and plenty of very unserious ones) and wondered why it never really happened. Then I met my husband and I understood. He will never let me forget that I told him on the first night we met that we were going to be together for ever and that I knew that he was the one I would finally be able to have babies with (yeah, I missed the 'play it cool' memo).

A conversation I had when I started in business is one that will always be firmly lodged in my brain. I was 30 and was speaking to a successful woman in her early 40s who had been head-down in business for the last 15 years.

'Be careful,' she said. 'One day you will look up from your laptop and you'll be in your 40s – and your best baby years will have passed you by.'

I smiled politely, thinking to myself smugly, 'Yeah ... that won't happen to me!'

Shortly after I met my husband, things with my first business became really stressful: toxic people dynamics, financial distress and general chaos leading to my eventual personal bankruptcy. One day I looked up from my laptop and I was indeed in my 40s and my best baby years had potentially passed me by.

Despite the chaos around us, we committed to beginning the process of 'trying', but I was overweight, with a BMI of 40+ and had fallen into some really unhealthy ways of managing stress, namely junk food and alcohol, with very little exercise (if any). So it was no real surprise that, despite our best efforts, it just wasn't happening for us.

Anyone who has been through this process will know how all-consuming that two-week cycle becomes, a series of peeing on sticks, using various gadgets that all promise to work miracles, taking temperatures and obsessively reading everything the algorithm thinks is useful to you in your quest to create human life.

And every time the test came back the same: 'Not pregnant.'

And so would begin the next phase of the two-week cycle, the one that no one sees, the conversation between me and me:

'What's wrong with you? This is all you've ever wanted.'

'Just eat less and move more.'

'If you won't lose weight to have a baby, then what will you do it for?'

'You obviously just don't want it enough.'

I didn't know at the time that I had ADHD, so I had no idea of the ways my brain was working against me, or how to work with it.

One of my favourite books is *The Chimp Paradox* by Dr Steve Peters.[15] *The Chimp Paradox* is not about ADHD brains specifically, but the chimp brain Dr Peters refers to is the limbic system, which is responsible for impulsivity, emotional reactions and short-term thinking. In the ADHD brain, where the prefrontal cortex is underdeveloped, the limbic system is overactive, so the chimp brain he is talking about relates to all the things we struggle with most with ADHD.

I found an article in which Dr Peters talked about working with the England football squad and cautioning the management and coaching team against using consequences as motivation to win big games.[16] He explained how, despite common misconception, the bigger the goal, the less motivated we become to achieve it. This is largely down to several factors:

- Overwhelm: large rewards can create pressure, leading to anxiety and avoidance behaviours.
- Disconnect: if the reward feels too distant, the 'chimp brain', with all its connections to impulsivity, may not find it compelling, thus reducing motivation.
- Perceived threat: high-stakes rewards can be interpreted as threats, triggering stress responses that hinder performance.

Once I read this, it all made sense. I was being so mean to myself, setting the biggest of prizes, the thing that meant the most to me in the world – OF COURSE I was overwhelmed. OF COURSE my body and brain shut down and didn't want to play.

This realisation was around the time I started to become aware of adult ADHD, and the fact that it could be the answer to my lifelong question of 'what is wrong with me?', and this chimp-shaped unlock, along with the new knowledge I had of my brain, changed my approach to baby-making in the strangest way. It allowed me to take the pressure off, be kinder to myself and actually listen to my body. I spent time alone, reflecting, and through that realised something *huge*.

I realised that I never actually wanted to be pregnant at all. Yes, I wanted a baby (desperately), but I had a deep-rooted and unaddressed fear of pregnancy linked to baby loss in my family when I was a child.

This realisation prompted a very deep conversation with my husband and we decided to adopt. Instantly. There was no back and forth, no 'what ifs', just an instant, bear-hug-from-the-universe, gut-affirming and unanimous 'this is the right thing for us'.

And my God ... it really was.

Apologies for the overshare, I know you didn't buy this book to hear about the inner workings of my womb, but learning such a huge lesson through such an important life experience shaped the way I set goals for ever. I became so much kinder to myself. It wasn't a case of being 'soft', or unambitious, but rather truly working *with* my brain to achieve the things that matter, in a way that works for both my brain and me.

I didn't realise it then, but this life-changing realisation helped me see – for the first time – that there really is more than one way to achieve a goal, in business or in life. So now, whenever I hear that bullying voice piping up inside, taunting me with the idea of not hitting my goals because I 'don't want them enough', I just look at my beautiful son and remember to be a bit kinder to myself.

Your Brain First business: The Brain First goal filter

So, we've accepted that our way of engaging with goals may differ from the norm, and we've let go of any shame and guilt attached to that. Now it's time to look at how we make sure we create future goals that work with our brains and not against them. Below you'll find a step-by-step guide to writing Brain First goals, any time you need them.

Use this when setting a goal to make sure it's aligned with what motivates you.

1. **What's the goal you're setting?**
Write it clearly, even if it feels vague right now
For example: Make more money

---

2. **Why do you want this?**
Keep asking yourself 'why?' until you hit the real emotional driver (it should feel meaningful, or even a bit uncomfortable)
For example: Because I'm scared I'm not really very good at this and I want to make what money I can before I'm 'found out'

---

3. **Is this a fear or desire?**
Which one is primarily driving you right now?
☐ I'm moving away from something I fear (e.g. failure, rejection, financial pressure)
☐ I'm moving towards something I desire (e.g. freedom, growth, purpose)
The goal is to be driven by desire, not fear. If you ticked fear, is there a version of this goal that's rooted in desire instead?
For example: I want to have more security for the future.

---

4. **Energy check**
On a scale of 1–10 (where 1 is demoralising and 10 is highly engaging):
How energising does this goal feel? ___ / 10
What might make it feel lighter or more appealing?
For example: If I have enough of a float, I could buy the car I have my eye on.

---

5. Know your motivators

Tick your top 1–2 natural motivators:

- ☐ Novelty/interest: I'm motivated by trying something new
- ☐ Problem solving: I'm motivated by finding answers to difficult problems
- ☐ Achievement: I'm motivated by hitting goals and being celebrated
- ☐ Growth: I'm motivated by being better than I was yesterday
- ☐ Connection: I'm motivated by interpersonal relationships and networking
- ☐ Autonomy: I'm motivated by being able to think and work independently
- ☐ Impact/Purpose: I'm motivated when I know what I'm doing has value
- ☐ Recognition/Status: I'm motivated by external approval, admiration and validation

Reflect on your original goal. Think of ways that you can weave in these motivators.

---

6. Reframe the goal

Now rework the goal to be Brain First and linked to your own motivators.

For example, my original goal in this example was 'Make more money'. I now know this is because I want more security and that I'm particularly galvanised by the idea of being able to buy a new car. If I've reflected that I'm primarily motivated by problem solving, a reworked 'make more money' goal might be 'Identify business efficiencies that allow me to increase profit'. If achievement also inspires me, putting measurable targets in place may help again, making a final goal: 'Identify business efficiencies that allow me to increase profit by 20 per cent by the end of the year.'

Now, over to you to apply the same logic:

Original goal: ____

Revised goal: ____

Reframing what you thought you knew

As with planning, goal setting isn't one thing that is done one way. The most important thing about setting a goal is that the pathway and destination are clear *to you* and that it feels achievable *to you*.

TL;DR

Negative consequences aren't motivating to us – because of our now/not now thinking, anything that will impact future us isn't happening.

Goals can easily fall into that category, so you need to find a way to motivate yourself that works.

The worst thing you can do is set goals that you can't achieve.

7

Working with people

When it takes a village to deliver your vision

Building a team can be crucial for business success, but managing one can be uniquely challenging for someone with ADHD.

Having supported hundreds of ADHD business owners, I know that one of the biggest challenges they come up against is working with people.

For some, that's because communication is exhausting when you have a brain that goes a million miles an hour and your mouth doesn't always keep up. It's yet another paradox of ADHD, because while the stereotype has us painted as hyper-active extroverts, that is rarely the case. It's true that you might see me or another ADHD founder being extroverted at times, but as you may well know from your own experience, we heavily pay the price for that later because all the 'jazz hands' behaviour is masking, and it's very draining.

For others, it might stem from a lifetime of always feeling a bit different. I remember seeing a post on LinkedIn saying that being easy to work with is an underrated career strategy, and while the initial comments were all nodding in virtual agreement and clapping hands, fairly soon people waded in with 'I'm neurodivergent and have always been told I'm difficult to work with'. I think conversations like this, acknowledging and making the case for difference, are really important to have, especially if we are to change attitudes in the workplace. We need to think beyond the behaviours that are commonly celebrated and accommodate people who get the work done without trying to win the office popularity contest.

As I mentioned in Part I, there is a popular phrase in the business world: 'go fast alone, go far together'. This phrase wasn't written with the ADHD brain in mind because given the choice, I know that the vast majority of us would choose to go fast alone. But if you do want to 'go far together', even if it doesn't come to you instinctively, it's perfectly possible. You *can* build a successful team – the truth is that, like every other area of building your Brain First business, it's about understanding what works for you and creating ways to make that happen daily.

If you need to grow a team to fulfil your business dreams, then read on to learn how you can do that in a way that works for you.

So, what's going on? The ADHD connection

Building a team can be crucial for business success, but managing one can be uniquely challenging for someone with ADHD because of how ADHD affects executive function, emotional regulation, attention and other skills.

Let's take a look at why.

EXECUTIVE FUNCTION CHALLENGES AND WORKING IN A TEAM

- Delegating is hard: you might think 'It's quicker if I do it myself' or struggle to break down tasks clearly for others.
- Planning and prioritising: managing timelines, check-ins and workload distribution can feel overwhelming without strong systems.
- Follow-through: we often get excited about the start of things but lose momentum when it comes to managing the middle or end (like performance reviews or feedback processes).

EMOTIONAL DYSREGULATION AND WORKING IN A TEAM

- Rejection sensitivity: giving and receiving feedback can feel intensely personal. You might avoid difficult conversations to protect yourself from discomfort.
- People-pleasing: you may become too emotionally involved, wanting to be liked rather than respected as a leader.

- Burnout from people management: you might give too much of yourself, overcompensating for internalised shame or masking.

ATTENTION DYSREGULATION AND WORKING IN A TEAM

- Inconsistent engagement: hyperfocus might mean you forget to check in with your team, or you're distracted and not fully present when they need you.
- Context-switching: managing multiple people's needs while juggling your own projects can feel like mental chaos.

IMPATIENCE AND FRUSTRATION AND WORKING IN A TEAM

- Different speeds: ADHD brains move fast, often expecting others to keep up, leading to frustration if they don't.
- Control issues: if things aren't done *your* way or fast enough, you may take back control, which undermines trust and autonomy.

INCONSISTENT SYSTEMS AND WORKING IN A TEAM

- Consistency: you may start using tools or processes to help manage your team but struggle to maintain them consistently. This creates confusion for team members who need predictability and structure.

Let's hear from someone who has hit these problems and overcome them, then we'll focus on the practical steps you can take to do the same.

Lucy's Brain First journey

Lucy Menghini didn't set out to build a fast-growing bridal brand. In fact, for most of her early life, she wasn't sure where she was headed at all.

'I always thought I wasn't smart enough, not thin enough, not pretty enough ... just not enough,' she told me.

She left school with no university plans and fell into a management training scheme at UK supermarket chain Sainsbury's. It felt like winning the lottery: a full-time job at 18 for £21,000 a year. But what followed were years of quietly navigating working life with undiagnosed ADHD – feeling like she was either doing too much or not enough. As she moved on from Sainsbury's this became a pattern of leaping before looking, hustling without structure, reaching milestones and feeling ... nothing.

Everything changed when Lucy and her husband Ross launched Six Stories, a bridal brand that started with embroidery machines in their apartment and exploded into a multi-million-pound business. Growth came fast, and with it responsibility, structure and expectations.

Lucy admits she still struggles with structure. She procrastinates. She avoids hard conversations until the last minute. She forgets numbers and needs things colour-coded. But she also *feels* what the customer wants before they even know they want it. She can spot a hire within seconds of them walking in.

Meanwhile, Ross, Lucy's husband and CEO, is neurotypical. Where Lucy is people-focused and led by instinct, he's analytical, methodical and commercial. Together, they are a perfect pairing – and a live example of a Brain First partnership that works because it plays to *both* people's strengths. 'I'd still be making tutus in my spare bedroom at a loss if Ross didn't join when he did,' Lucy says. 'Ross absolutely is the growth – and I'm kind of like ... the shine!'

It wasn't until her ADHD diagnosis that Lucy gave herself permission to focus on the parts of the business that she's brilliant at and to trust her husband and wider team with the rest – and that's when everything started to click.

Now, rather than managing solo, she invites others in. She is radically honest with her team – she tells them when she's overwhelmed, when she can't focus and when she needs support instead of silence. 'If you need me to do something, sit me down and do it with me,' she tells them. It's not weakness, it's how she gets things done.

This is how Lucy and Ross divide things to make it work for them: he handles structure, scale, numbers; she brings intuition, creativity and everything 'brand'. Ross manages forecasts. Lucy casts the vision. Ross builds systems. Lucy makes decisions quickly – even if they're wrong – just to get the ball rolling.

'I'd rather make the wrong decision than spend hours discussing it – let's just try it and see ... whatever it is!'

That speed, instinct and customer obsession is what got Six Stories to £10 million in annual revenue. But Lucy doesn't pretend she could have done it alone – nor does she try to emulate how Ross works.

'There's no pretending. I'm not going to sit in a trade meeting and pretend I understand every number on the dashboard. That's not my zone of genius. I'll be replying to DMs instead.

'We're yin and yang,' Lucy says. 'I am impulsive, chaotic, feelings-first. He's detail-focused, calm and future-thinking. He'll be looking at CAC reports and profit forecasts and I'm like – sorry, no, I physically cannot.'

Instead of forcing herself into tasks that drain her energy or trigger overwhelm, Lucy has learnt to be unapologetically protective of her bandwidth, or 'buckets' as she calls them. 'I'm fiercely protective of my buckets. I know if I dip into the work bucket, it will take energy away from the family bucket – and I get to make a conscious decision about that.'

There's no elaborate blueprint. No neatly colour-coded org chart. Just radical self-awareness, open communication and a willingness to say, 'I can't do this right now' without guilt or shame.

And perhaps most importantly, a shared belief that different brains bring different brilliance.

Lucy's story isn't about getting everything right. It's about someone *finally understanding what's right for her.*

Knowledge is power when it comes to our challenges. Just because we find these things hard doesn't mean they're not possible. Half the battle is understanding what is going on and, like Lucy has done, being vulnerable enough to trust your team and to lead them in a way that feels authentic to you.

I spent far too long cosplaying a neurotypical leader when I had big teams and it was no good for anyone: it led to inconsistency and confusion for them, and a cycle of never-ending burnout for me.

There are so many ways to build a team these days, it really doesn't have to look like bums on seats. It could be a remote team of contractors or virtual assistants, it could be fractional support in a senior team, or it could be pulling teams together on a project basis to achieve a specific goal. And there are many ways to interact with that team and to inspire them.

For example, if you have identified that you really don't want to be tied to one location, then a remote team could well be the way to go. If you have a business that is seasonal and so you have fluctuating sales and need for resource, then definitely build a team of contractors. If you are someone who values working alone, find some really good specialists to tap into as and when you need them.

Getting really honest with yourself about how you work best, and what that needs to look like in your team, is the key to creating your Brain First business.

Your Brain First business: How to delegate

We've talked about trusting your team in the previous pages, but how do you get to the point where you feel you can do that?

Delegation is hugely important in effective team building and yet it's one of the areas which people I have worked with struggle the most.

BARRIERS TO DELEGATION

Before we get into the exercise, rather than doing our usual trick of jumping in both feet first, let's take a moment to understand where you actually need alignment in this area. This is a really important step as we want to make sure you are treating the cause here, not just the symptom.

So, take a moment to consider the following (be as honest as you can):

'This feels like too much'
Rooted in: executive function struggles

- Do you find it hard to get your thoughts clear enough to explain what you want someone to do?
- Does the process of writing a brief or explaining a task feel overwhelming or too 'energy expensive'?
- Do you avoid delegating because it feels quicker or easier to do it yourself?
- How often do you delay delegating because you're not 'ready' or don't have everything worked out?
- Do you not trust yourself to follow up on tasks you've delegated?

'I'll just do it myself'
Rooted in: control/perfectionism

- Do you believe no one can do the task as well as you?
- Do you worry that delegating will result in mistakes that you'll then have to fix?

- Does it frustrate you when things aren't done your way or on your timeline?
- Do you secretly enjoy the adrenaline of being the one who saves the day?

'I don't want to bother them'
Rooted in: people-pleasing or emotional discomfort

- Do you feel guilty asking people for help or support?
- Do you worry that delegating will make people like you less?
- Do you avoid giving feedback or corrections after delegating because it feels awkward or 'mean'?
- Are you afraid of being seen as lazy, demanding or a 'bad boss'?

'I have to do everything here'
Rooted in: self-concept and identity

- Do you tie your worth or identity to being the one who 'does it all'?
- Do you struggle to trust that others are as committed or capable as you?
- Does delegating make you feel as though you're giving up control or relevance?

'I'm sure I'll have time'
Rooted in: time management and energy miscalculations

- Do you underestimate how long a task will take and assume you can squeeze it in?
- Do you tell yourself 'it'll only take me five minutes' even if that's rarely true?
- Do you feel you have to be at full capacity before asking for help?
- Do you struggle with identifying or expressing your needs?

'It's just easier this way'

Rooted in: past experiences or fear of conflict

- Have you had bad experiences where delegation didn't work out?
- Do you avoid delegating because you're unsure how to handle it if someone lets you down?
- Do you associate delegation with confrontation, correction or disappointment?

Taking the time to understand where your resistance to delegation is rooted won't cure it overnight, but it will help you identify the area you need to focus on in your alignment process and also to understand that it's not that you are 'bad at delegating': there is a root cause and a belief that you are holding onto which is currently self-fulfilling, i.e. you believe it, so you don't delegate and never get the chance to prove yourself wrong.

SUCCESSFUL DELEGATION

I use this simple template when delegating to get clear on the task myself and then give that clarity to anyone else involved. Without that clarity, you are setting them up to fail (and I don't know what your answers are to the questions above, but maybe that is subconsciously why you're doing it?).

It works as a repeatable Notion doc, Google Doc or PDF template. You can voice-record this as well if written tasks feel heavy.

Step	Task details	Notes
Name the task	e.g. Send out the weekly newsletter using last week's podcast episode	
What does 'done' look like?	e.g. Email is scheduled for Thursday 3 pm with the correct link and no typos	
Deadline (realistic and specific)	e.g. Thursday at 12 pm	
Preferred format	e.g. Draft in Google Doc, then uploaded and ready to go in [preferred tool] ... or even 'I trust your format – just let me know when done'	
Check-in point	e.g. Check in on Wednesday; send draft/outline before doing the full thing; add to our central doc for review ... or even 'no check-in necessary'	
Linked resources	e.g. Please find attached a link to the podcast episode; our brand style guide; call to action to use	
Final ADHD prompt	e.g. Is there anything in my head I haven't said yet? Write or voice note it	

I'd also recommend that you ask everyone in your team to use a template like this when a task needs to be completed. This will give everyone clarity on the task, expectations and timeline and it's a really big step towards Brain First team work.

Reframing what you thought you knew

Building a team isn't about losing autonomy or multiplying your headaches – it should be the opposite. A well-built team, hired for your weaknesses and given clear direction, will always help you grow faster.

Start by getting to know your own limiting beliefs around team work and delegation, then challenge them as you grow.

TL;DR

Building a team isn't the only way to grow a business, but it can be rewarding and reap dividends if you find a way to work with people that suits everyone.

8

Keeping the changes

Being consistent and staying on track, even when you start feeling lost

> **Consistency is whatever you can manage on your worst day or week.**

We're nearly at the end of the alignment section and you should be getting a good understanding of what changes you want to make to make sure your business practices are as 'you-oriented' as possible.

But making plans is one thing, sticking to them consistently is another. Old habits die hard and when you have brains as complicated and full of paradoxes as ours, it's a real challenge to maintain *any* change, no matter how beneficial it may be. In this chapter we'll be looking at the best way to stay on track so you keep coming back to your Brain First business even when the world is telling you a million other ways you 'should' be working.

The online definition of a habit is 'a regularly repeated behaviour that is often performed without conscious thought'.[17] I mean, I don't know about you, but going by that, I'm not sure I have ever had a habit in my whole life. With the exception of eating snacks when I'm watching TV, I feel like I have to consciously think about *everything* I do.

We know that ADHD brains crave novelty, urgency and immediate reward, which is what makes traditional habit-building so painful; habits rely on consistency and delayed gratification, but we run on interest and stimulation. It's not that we can't build habits, we just need to do it differently – with variety, quick/visible wins and a process that can flex with our brains and doesn't try to keep them in a cage.

However, I also think it's really helpful to know that new habits aren't easy for anyone – the most neurotypical person in the world would struggle to form a new habit. Sure, they might find it easier to follow a plan to get things started, but they would still find it hard making the habit a regularly repeated behaviour that is performed without conscious thought. So, that's the first thing: let's not kid ourselves that this is going to be straightforward.

If it's tough for neurotypicals, it's doubly tough for us with our brains that would rather stick with the painful but familiar than make the effort to change. For ADHD brains, change is loaded with effort, risk and the stories we tell ourselves. Familiar might be painful, but at least it's predictable – and that feels safe.

The worst thing is, we just love to make stuff hard for ourselves. The ADHD brain is often predisposed to all-or-nothing binary thinking, so no matter how much you know that the best way to approach making change is with baby steps, altering one thing at a time, there's every likelihood that you will still read this book making promises to yourself that the day after you finish it you'll have a whole new approach to business and nothing will ever be difficult again.

Well, I hate to break it to you but that 'flick of a switch' change just isn't going to happen.

Those big changes we make, like:

- joining the gym and deciding you're going to be that person from now on
- buying everything you need for a new hobby and promising yourself this time you will actually use it
- signing up for a course or new piece of software for your business and swearing this will change your life ...

Those big pledges? They never last, and worse than that, they kick off a net-negative cycle of shame and diminished self-trust.

Take the gym-going example. Does the following sound familiar?

- You wake up feeling tired and out of shape.
- You decide to sign up for the gym.
- You buy some new trainers online.
- You tell your family and friends you've joined the gym and yeah it's pricey, but you've worked out that if you go just

five times a week then it's actually very good value for money.

- You manage to go three times in the first week and share your victory on social media, trying not to sound as smug as you feel.
- Week two you go twice.
- Week three you don't go at all.
- When you see friends, they say how great it is you're going to the gym.
- Your family start asking how your five-times-a-week-fancy-gym is.
- The gym starts sending 'we miss you – come back!' emails.
- Your membership fee continues to come out of the bank for the next 12 months.
- You end up feeling worse than you did before you signed up because now you've broken another promise to yourself, your family have another reason to laugh when you share your new big idea with them – and you're a couple of grand worse off.

So, let's agree at this point that all-or-nothing, big promises are not good for us. Ok?

So, what's going on? The ADHD connection

One of the (many) paradoxes of ADHD is that although we're big-picture thinkers and can visualise the business and where we want it to be, once we're in the weeds of the day-to-day of it, it's very hard for us to hold the macro and micro visions at the same time. So it's common for us to look up one day and realise we have veered so far off track that we've gone from the core business that made us so happy to a completely different version that we don't even recognise.

With our golden retriever energy, it's easy for us to have an idea, sell a bit, grow a bit, sell a bit, grow a bit more – and end up in a place we didn't even know existed, let alone set out to get to. When aligning our business to our strengths, we need to be absolutely intentional about our growth or our people-pleasing, FOMO, and never-ending need to 'prove' ourselves that will find us right back in a business that works for everyone – apart from us.

As you'll hear repeatedly in this book: for your business to work, *it has to work for you* – not the other way round.

There are some common traps you can fall into along the way when building your business, particularly when tapping into external expertise in the form of online resources, self-proclaimed 'gurus', or perhaps even genuine experts. Until fairly recently, all advice was presented as equal. There was no distinction between neurotypical and neurodivergent advice (and there isn't always now), but it's important to distinguish between the advice that will work for you and the advice that won't – otherwise you end up wasting time, money and energy following tips and tricks that just make you feel a hundred times worse about yourself because they are based on a whole different operating system to the one you are working with.

Some of the common (neurotypical-friendly) advice we're told to follow that makes it hard for ADHD brains to stay on track includes:

- You should work a 'neurotypical' week: who says the working day is 9–5 and the working week is Monday to Friday? It's your business, you get to work the hours that work for you (and your brain!). Understanding your own energy flow is the key to getting this right for you – regardless of whether you have a team or not, nailing this is so important.
- Your success should look a particular way: year-on-year growth and ever-increasing targets work for corporates reporting to their shareholders, but do they really work for you? Maybe you came from a corporate background and believe that this is how you *should* do things. Well, here's a shoulder dropper for you: it isn't!
- You have things to do just 'because you should': our brains need to understand *why* we are doing something. We struggle to follow arbitrary rules or processes, so when we are creating forecasts that feel like we are just making up a load of numbers on a spreadsheet, or writing a strategy because it's what we see other people do, it can play all kinds of tricks with our brain – and you really don't need to fall into that trap.

If ADHD has taught us anything it's that we are experts at being consistently inconsistent. Having the framework for your Brain First business is a guide to keep you on track, but ADHD means that you will naturally gravitate towards old habits. If (when!) that happens, don't beat yourself up. Recognise that you are falling back into your old ways and course correct.

If I see one more 'expert' saying that the key to success is consistency, I might just rip my eyeballs out. It's not that they are wrong, it's that they often equate consistency with showing up at 100 per cent every single day, and that isn't how we should be thinking about consistency.

I don't know if you were in business through the late 2010s, but the rise of bro culture online sounded like: WAKE UP AT 4 AM! HUSTLE HARD! DREAM BIGGER! MAKE MORE MONEY! SLEEP WHEN YOU'RE DEAD! It only took a few years for this message to change to: I've actually realised there is more to life; I now wear a ring to make sure I'm getting enough sleep; balance is so important; have you tried meditation? You will still see pockets of the toxic hustle brigade online, but largely (and mentioning no names) they realised that this just wasn't sustainable – even when you're in your early 20s.

There is no law that says you need to be consistent – let's get that clear to start with. But where you do want to set a habit, it doesn't mean operating at full throttle no matter what – you can be consistent in smaller ways and at your own pace ... and without the 'big promises'.

You might already know this as a concept, but I want you to read this a few times and really absorb it: *consistency is steadily doing whatever you can manage on your worst day/week.*

Let's take social media activity because that seems to be an area where we beat ourselves up most about consistency. The reality is that:

- consistency for you might look like one post a day, one post a week or one post a month
- it's an effort doomed to fail to try to be a post-a-day person if you are realistically a post-a-week person.

As someone who has grown a fairly decent-sized audience online, I can tell you that the most important thing about your content is energy. If you're creating and posting from a place of 'Argh, I need to post something – that will do', then it's highly unlikely to achieve the objective you are working towards.

So, consistency in your content is like consistency across your business:

- Understand what you're trying to achieve.
- Be honest about the time/energy/focus you can give it.
- Set your goal accordingly.

Small, realistic, 'one foot in front' steps are better than crazy visionary ones that soak up more energy than you have to spare.

Laura's Brain First journey: Maintaining balance

Laura Jackson didn't set out to build a business. She set out to follow her curiosity. What unfolded across supper clubs, TV, homewares and more was a career stitched together with intuition, creativity and a deep-rooted belief in the power of community.

Raised in the joyful chaos of a blended family, Laura learnt early how to navigate group dynamics, make space for everyone and build connection in unpredictable environments, all while having fun. 'There'd be ten of us around the table for tea after school,' she says. 'I didn't realise it at the time, but that kind of togetherness shaped everything I've built since.'

School, however, was not her happy place. With ADHD and dyslexia, Laura struggled with traditional education. 'I couldn't remember anything, couldn't write properly, just felt crap,' she says. 'But I knew I liked people and I knew I wanted to do something different.'

That 'something different' led her to start a supper club. And what began as a passion project reminiscent of those family afternoons became a seven-year whirlwind of joyful, raucous evenings bringing strangers together around food and conversation. It was community in its most delicious form, and it snowballed fast. Brand collaborations, product lines and a media profile followed. But when that chapter ended, Laura didn't flinch. She built something new, this time a homewares marketplace called Glassette.

Alongside it all, she continued to juggle media work, partnerships and creative projects. She's built a team that she trusts and now leans into her creative zone, signing off on visuals, nurturing brand relationships and staying out of the spreadsheets. 'I still beat myself up that I can't sit in data meetings without zoning out. But then I remember – my strength is the big ideas, the instinct, the network, the energy. That's where I add value.'

Her ADHD isn't something she tries to fix, it's something she's built around. 'People always say, "You've got so much energy", but when you really love what you do, it doesn't feel like work. And with this brain, downtime is hard anyway. So I just keep going – but on my terms.'

Her biggest learning? That traditional business blueprints don't work for everyone. And in the creative world, they often don't apply at all.

'Business doesn't have to look like pencil skirts and London or New York offices. You can build something beautiful, something meaningful, by doing it your way. And for me, that means people first, always. Relationships, community, collaboration – everything good has come from that.'

When we speak, Laura reminds me of one of the most underrated pieces of life advice: 'It's just not that deep,' she says. And instantly my shoulders drop and my jaw unclenches. Laura doesn't need to justify her creativity – it *is* the business. From product launches to partnerships, her instincts and ideas are her biggest strategic assets. She's happy to do things differently, to do it her way and to make sure fun isn't a bonus – it's baked into the business model. And the consequence? She maintains balance and avoids burnout. It's absolutely a win:win.

Your Brain First business: How to overcome blocks and avoid the return to bad habits

EXERCISE: THE RESET ROADMAP

1. RECOGNISE THE SHIFT

Write down the three biggest signs that tell you you're slipping back into bad habits.

(Examples: overfilling your calendar, saying yes too often, chasing shiny ideas, people-pleasing.)

2. SPOT THE SIGNS

For each, ask: What's really behind this?

- Fear (of letting people down, of missing out)
- Habit (defaulting to what you've always done)
- Energy (your brain is overloaded)

Circle the one that fits each.

3. APPLY THE BRAIN FIRST FILTER

Go through your current workload and put each task into one of these buckets:

- Eliminate – say no, let go or delete
- Delegate – outsource or co-create
- Automate – do it in fewer steps, automate or time-box
- Concentrate – it energises you and drives impact

4. RESET YOUR VISION

Remind yourself what your Brain First business looks like.

- How does your business feel (compared to how it currently feels)?
- How many hours a day feels good?
- When is your natural focus/low-energy time?
- What tasks are only done on certain days (batching, time-blocking)?

5. CHOOSE YOUR RESET RULE

Pick one rule that prevents the old habits creeping back.

(Examples: 'No meetings on Mondays.' 'Only two offers at a time.' 'Admin is always delegated.')

6. ANCHOR STATEMENT

Write one sentence that becomes your 'reset anchor' when things feel too much. Print it out, stick it on your screen, tattoo it to your forehead!

(Example: 'My business works best when I do less ... better.')

Reframing what you thought you knew

Success isn't something that happens as a result of a few small changes, a new hire or an updated process, it's a culmination of all those things, and more. Get out of binary, black-and-white thinking and allow yourself the time, space and grace to grow.

TL;DR

Old habits die hard, don't expect changes to happen overnight.

Accept that consistency is whatever you can achieve on your worst day or week.

Just putting one foot in front of the other is often the answer.

9

Getting to grips with risk and failure

> **Failure is data, not a verdict. It's how we learn, test, adjust and grow. But ADHD brains often struggle to separate 'I failed' from 'I am a failure'. That's where the real pain sits.**

The cupcake business I started in 2007 ended in 2014 in personal bankruptcy. The thought of a cute, pink cupcake brand serving tea out of vintage china ending in bankruptcy is crazy, but that is what happened.

I had taken on a unit in a local shopping centre and had been told that because of the location of the unit, there would be no business rates to pay. I based my forecasts and decisions on that information and took the huge leap of opening a store there. Even with my plans in place, I knew I was taking a financial risk – but I wanted to do it anyway.

One day I turned up to find someone very official-looking measuring the unit. A few weeks later I received a bill for over £60,000 in arrears and £40,000 per year going forward.

That's a whole load of extra cupcakes to sell!

And there began my long, painful journey to failure – most of it spent with me desperately clinging on, arranging payment plans on payment plans and kidding myself that we could make it through. Until one day, I just had to admit that we couldn't.

I still have some conflicting feelings around accountability and responsibility for this, and while I take full responsibility for the outcome of the business, I was missold the lease and regret not fighting it at the time, but I just didn't have any fight left in me.

I have a high propensity for risk and before I knew that was because of ADHD, I never even stopped to question it.

I left my job during one of the worst recessions in our lifetime.

I moved out of my mortgaged home to a rental with no plan because I wanted a change of scenery.

I've taken on commercial leases I couldn't afford on paper, committed to events I wasn't confident I could deliver and made plans I knew I didn't have the skills to execute.

All in the knowledge I would 'work it out'.

Of course, willingness to take risks isn't the same for everyone with ADHD (and indeed, individual appetites for risk-taking will vary for each of us depending on the situation and our energy levels). This chapter is about exploring risk – figuring out how to make it work for us so we don't jump in feet first every time, but equally so we don't end up paralysed by a fear of failure.

Because risk can be a brilliant thing. Trusting your instinct and allowing it to guide you in your entrepreneurial journey can be absolutely key. I haven't met a single successful business owner who doesn't regret some of their decisions along the way, but I have met plenty of unsuccessful or unfulfilled ones who have doubted their instincts and not taken necessary risks.

So, what's going on? The ADHD connection

People with ADHD can be particularly comfortable with risk and that's because of how our brains process reward impulse and novelty. It's not that we consciously enjoy risk more, it's that we're wired to respond differently to stimulation and consequences.

Here's a quick breakdown of why that happens.

HIGH NOVELTY-SEEKING

ADHD brains have lower baseline levels of dopamine, the neurotransmitter linked to reward and motivation. Risky or novel situations (starting a business, impulsive decisions, trying something new) can give a quick dopamine hit – making our brains feel temporarily more alive, engaged or focused. In brief, risk equals reward is a shortcut for a dopamine-hungry brain.

IMPULSE OVER INHIBITION

The prefrontal cortex (which helps with planning and inhibition) is often underactive in ADHD brains. This makes it harder to pause and think through consequences – not because we don't care but because our brain is wired for action first, reflection later.

WEIGHING LONG-TERM VS SHORT-TERM

Remember that time-blindness we talked about? People with ADHD may struggle to prioritise long-term consequences over short-term excitement or urgency. This can make risks seem smaller or more worth it in the moment – you might recognise this as the 'F it, why not?' way of thinking.

ADAPTATION TO UNCERTAINTY

Many people with ADHD are used to things not going as planned, so we get better at adapting, recovering from mistakes and operating in chaos. This can make us feel more comfortable with risk because we know we can figure it out as we go. It becomes our baseline.

The problems can kick in when all that risk-taking leads to a heap of failures. When we get burnt, fear of failure can kick in, raising a whole new heap of other issues.

Fear of failure isn't just a mindset issue – it's a brain response, especially for those of us with ADHD. It's not about laziness, low confidence, or lack of ambition. It's often about overwhelm, emotional intensity and experiences that taught us failure equals danger.

Here are some of the reasons we tend to fear failure:

- Emotional regulation is harder. Small setbacks can feel huge.
- RSD means criticism (even imagined or perceived) cuts deep.

- We struggle to picture the steps, so our brain jumps straight to the worst-case scenario.
- Experiences of being told we were 'too much' or 'not enough' fuel shame spirals.

We can easily become trapped in the self-fulfilling fear loop, which looks something like this:

> Fear → Perfectionism → Procrastination → Shame → Avoidance → More Fear

Once we've hit this point, we need to work hard to break the cycle and get our risk-taking mojo back (within reason).

My Brain First journey: Learning to fail

Failure is such a funny word in business. I don't mean rib-popping funny, I mean that there are so many different interpretations of the experience. In the UK, we talk about it with the kind of reverence usually reserved for funerals, while in the US it's worn as a badge of honour – success is just the outcome of a string of failures, right?

Just a few years after I went through bankruptcy in my business, I was invited on a trip to New Zealand for a few months. There was a mixture of British, American, Canadian, Australian and New Zealand business owners there and I was still in the habit of trying to skirt around the topic of my failure for fear of judgement. As we were there for some time, I eventually shared my story and to my surprise was instantly elevated to the most experienced, celebrated and respected person in the room.

Instead of the sad faces and awkward questions I expected I was met with:

'Wow, what an experience!'

'You must have learnt so much to take forward into this business.'

'Tell me everything!'

That moment healed something inside me and helped me see that the way we respond to the thing that happened is not only *all* we have control over but is also the most impactful way of controlling what happens next.

I listened to a podcast recently[18] where the guest was talking about being sent to jail for six-and-a-half years because he couldn't pay a huge tax bill his business was liable for. Despite agreeing to a plan to repay the $5 MILLION, the IRS had swept his account of all funds and contacted his clients to alert them to the situation, leaving him with a collapsed business overnight.

The story itself was fascinating (and terrifying in equal measure!) but there was something else about it that had me absolutely gripped – the way he was able to reflect on this failure with humour and a clear sense of which bit of it was his to own and which bit wasn't.

This isn't something I am great at, and – sweeping generalisation alert – I see this a lot with women, especially neurodivergent women. Our diminished sense of self-trust, the negative voices we hear growing up and the fact that girls are four times more likely to go undiagnosed with ADHD than boys[19] all contribute to fragile self-esteem and us living our lives under a cloud of apology.

So when failure hits and we are finally proven right – 'I knew it! I AM useless!' – where men might rationally assess the situation, we tend to scurry away in shame and berate ourselves, making up false stories about what this means about who we are as a person.

This loop keeps us stuck – not because we're unmotivated, but because our nervous system is in survival mode. This is just another route we love to take to burnout and is so familiar to many of us that we don't even consciously recognise it any more.

My mum and dad have a saying – you know the way parents do? Well, if I ever complain about anything, they respond: 'Good or bad, who can say?'

I use this logic when I think about my experiences with 'failure'. Of course I wish I had never gone through bankruptcy and wish I had had the strength and gumption at the time to fight it, but had I not gone through that, then perhaps I would have a national cupcake retail chain or franchise business (and I genuinely couldn't think of anything less suited to my brain than that). I almost certainly wouldn't be doing what I'm doing today, and that realisation brings me great comfort.

Your Brain First business: The fear finder exercise

So how do we become ok with failure or right ourselves after a setback? The first step is to remind ourselves that it's part of doing business to feel confident enough to take calculated risks in the first place. To help with that, I suggest running through the following process when the self-doubt gremlins come to play.

1. Name the fear: What am I actually afraid of?
   → 'I'll embarrass myself' / 'People won't take me seriously' / 'I'll prove I can't do this'
2. Trace it back: Where did that belief come from?
   → A past failure? A comment from school? A parent's expectation?
3. Spot the pattern: How does this fear show up in my business?
   → Overplanning, avoiding decisions, quitting halfway through

I find just going through this process helps to heal some of the fear and shame we hold around failure. Then the next step is to start reframing some of those stories you have been telling yourself. This will help you move forward with a more positive mindset.

Here are a few examples for you to start with. Try to add some more of your own.

Old thought	**Brain First reframe**
'I messed it up.'	'I experimented.'
'This didn't work.'	'Now I know what to try next.'
'I shouldn't have tried.'	'Trying is what gets me unstuck.'
'I failed.'	'I made progress I can't measure yet.'

Remember, you're not here to succeed without failing. You're here to learn how to keep going when things get uncomfortable.

Reframing what you thought you knew

Success and failure are two sides of the same coin: if you are afraid of failure, you almost certainly won't reach the level of success you are aiming for.

What is failure anyway? It's just a series of brave decisions that you took that didn't work out and gave you experience and knowledge to take with you.

TL;DR

Our appetite for risk is a double-edged sword: it can lead us to failure, but it is also the secret to our success.

The key is in learning how to trust your instinct while tempering your impulses.

We've internalised failure as proof that we're not good enough, smart enough, or cut out for this. But what if failure was just ... part of it?

You're not scared of failing. You're scared of what you've made failure mean.

PART III

Action

Brain First you

Your guide to Part III

This section is where we make the magic happen. It's based on my professional and personal experience, along with deep research and learnings from working with hundreds of ADHD business owners, implementing the very strategies I share in the following section, with great success.

In each chapter, I break down a common ADHD challenge, take a look at the potential impact on your businesses, and offer some tried-and-tested strategies for you to add to your Brain First Toolkit.

HOW TO USE PART III

I designed this section as a pick'n'mix guide to support you in your Brain First journey. I know only too well how challenging it can be to consume a load of information and then *actually* put it into action, so you will notice each of these chapters is shorter than in the previous Parts. Although they outline the challenging trait or behaviour and why it's happening, they then get straight into strategies to help.

But before we get into guidance for specific problems, I want to offer some broader tips and tools that have helped me and my clients immensely but which don't necessarily belong in the chapters ahead.

GENERAL TIPS AND TOOLS

ARTIFICIAL INTELLIGENCE (AI)

Controversial and fear-inducing to many, but the dawn of AI has given us the level playing field we have been begging for: it allows us to shortcut time by preparing plans, fleshing out ideas and organising our thoughts. We can summarise volumes of information that otherwise we would find impossible to consume, all of which makes running our businesses so much easier.

AI is the fastest developing technology we have ever witnessed, and the rate that the big players are releasing new features and huge, meaningful updates is dizzying.

There are a number of things about AI that I feel deeply uncomfortable about – the issues around copyrighted material, how it will affect jobs in the future and the environmental impact – but I couldn't not include such a powerful tool in this book as I have seen and felt the benefits, both in my own business and in clients'.

Here is how I consciously use it to support my brain and business:

- Research
  - I use AI to research *everything*. I've used it for this book. It helps me collate important research and studies quickly, when previously it would have taken me hours trawling through search results to find the correct piece of information.
  - Note: AI for me is a starting point – *never an end point*. You will *never* see me copying and pasting from AI tools; I don't believe that is how we should be working if we are to nurture and enhance the uniqueness of our beautiful, squishy, creative brains. However, it shortcuts me to a point where I can assess information and decide what I want to progress with.
- Content
  - I have tasks set up to collate the most interesting news stories relating to business and ADHD across the globe. It lists them for me and pulls out the key points. This informs my content plan and my email newsletter.
  - Note: I do not get it to write my content, I get it to do the grunt work of researching and curating. This saves me time and energy that I can then put into the creativity of crafting a piece of content from the information provided.
- Clarification
  - If I have an idea but I need clarity on it, I will dump it down and get AI to untangle it, then repeat it back to me in a way that makes sense. As someone who finds communicating and delegating energy-expensive, this is a great way for me to pull things together independently.
  - Note: I do not then run away blindly with the response presented to me. Rather, I take it as a black-and-white,

unemotional summary of the information I put in, which I use to assess and plan what comes next.

- Tools
  - I use a number of AI tools that support me with meeting notes, email management and automations and I would be lost without them. I do have to watch my shiny object syndrome because it's easy to get dazzled by the new thing that comes along in such a fast-moving area of tech, but my advice is to find what works – and stick with it.
  - Note: none of these systems is failproof. Please do not set and forget; instead use them as tools to remove steps from your manual processes.

If you're going to use AI, my pleas to you are:

- Please do so consciously, and conscientiously, i.e. don't fall into the trap of chatting back and forth or generating a ton of work you will never actually use.
- Remain critical and creative. I have seen incredible, intelligent, highly qualified experts handing their credibility over to AI and killing their reputation in one LinkedIn post for the sake of automation. There are places to save time and there are places where it is very wisely spent, and in my opinion, anything that carries your reputation falls into the latter.

Remember, the goal isn't to hand over your entire personality to AI and exchange it for an excessive use of bullet points and rhetorical questions – the goal is to leverage your energy, shortcut your time and increase your *quality* of output.

BODY DOUBLING

Body doubling is one of my secret weapons in business and it always amazes me when people don't know about it, especially as they are usually doing it already in some way, they just don't realise that's what they are doing!

Body doubling is where you use the energy that comes from having someone else with you (virtually or physically) to get work done. This works differently for everyone. While some people are horrified by the idea of having anyone physically sitting with them while they work (me!), they may still find that they work best when they know someone is in the vicinity.

But what is the science behind this?

- Externalised accountability (social facilitation)
  - When someone else is present (even if they're not interacting with you), your brain perceives a kind of social pressure to stay on task. This taps into a psychological phenomenon called social facilitation, where performance improves simply because you're being observed (or think you are).
- Temporal anchoring and time perception
  - People with ADHD often struggle with time blindness – the inability to sense time passing or prioritise effectively. Body doubling provides a real-time anchor, helping your brain map time more concretely. 'We're starting at 10 am and working for 25 minutes' is more actionable than 'I need to do this today'.

- Nervous system co-regulation
  - When you're dysregulated or overwhelmed, having another calm, focused person present can help regulate your own nervous system. This is a technique that parents use with babies and toddlers and the need for co-regulation doesn't just disappear as we get older. This is especially true when tackling high-stress or emotionally charged tasks like admin or emails that you've been putting off too long.
- Executive function boost
  - Our brains struggle with task initiation, sequencing and motivation – core aspects of executive function. Body doubling helps bypass the initiation hurdle. The magic here lies in the fact you aren't deciding to start, you're simply following the group's or partner's momentum. It's a bit like hitching a ride on someone else's focus!
- Dopamine and novelty
  - Doing a normally boring task in a slightly novel way – like with a stranger on a video call or in a co-working group – can provide just enough dopamine stimulation and novelty to keep you engaged.

Here are some ways body doubling works and could work for you:

- Physical: this is where you need to sit with someone to work. I personally couldn't think of anything worse and know I would spend the whole time trying not to ask them what they watched on TV last night, but this works really well for some people and maybe it would work for you?
- Virtual: this is where you have one or more people on a video call and you all get on with your work. I find this kind

of body doubling really effective and it's helped me through many tasks that have been pushed down my to-do list for too many days in a row. You can either set this up with friends or find a group or platform that already offers this.

- Distanced: this is one that people often already use but don't realise it's what they are doing. A great example of this is working in a coffee shop. You're sitting alone, but the energy of people around you, and the change in environment, give you just enough dopamine to get through those tasks. This is a firm favourite of mine.
- Environmental: this again is one many people rely on without knowing it's a thing. I often hear this with people who work from home and struggle to work with anyone in the room with them but find it really helpful if someone is just there, somewhere in the house. If this is you then maybe you've only just realised that this is what you are doing and could try some of the other forms of body doubling if you struggle when there is no one around.

BUILD YOUR ALTER EGO

This one is weirdly controversial. When I speak about it online, people will say it's just masking, but it's not. Let me explain ...

Think of it like this: you don't see Beyoncé on stage – you see Sasha Fierce. Beyoncé described Sasha as 'the fun, more sensual, more aggressive, more outspoken, more glamorous side'[20] that emerges during performances, letting her separate her personal identity from her stage persona.

Building an alter ego is a powerful way of navigating the areas you find challenging in business, and indeed in life. This isn't about creating 'Sandra from Finance' so you can force yourself to fill out that spreadsheet or get stuck into your accounts (you need to know the areas you find challenging and navigate them with support), this is about creating a persona that embodies the energy you need to find in order to support your goals, then calling on it when you need it most.

Creating an alter ego can be a shortcut to finding the energy you need to show up online, do that presentation or send that email pitch – they are things that you want to do and will get you closer to your goals, you just need to borrow some of that Sasha Fierce energy to do it.

Start by thinking of the energy you're looking to summon – I like to think of it as the very best version of me. On those days when I'm feeling hormonal, tired or when self-doubt has won, I can call on my alter ego and borrow the energy of the very best version of me for a while.

Let's face it, Sasha Fierce doesn't do the school run and Beyoncé doesn't perform at the Super Bowl. Right?

UNHINGED TACTICS

Here are some of the more chaotic strategies that I keep in my back pocket for when nothing else is working:

- Going to a coffee shop to work with 40 per cent battery and no charger: this is my go-to strategy when I'm struggling to get my brain to co-operate. The distanced body doubling, battery-danger dopamine and time limit just set my brain on fire! Try it.

- That five minutes before an online call: I know I'm not alone in this one – I can get more done in that five minutes before a scheduled call than I can for the whole rest of the day.
- Danger work: someone offered this genius expression in my comments once and I can't get it out of my head. This is when you know someone could interrupt you at any moment so you work fast just in case. This works well if you're working from home and know your mother-in-law likes to pop in 'for a chat', or if you're in the office, try jumping in a meeting room you didn't book.
- Working in my car: something about the solitude and the safe environment makes my car one of my favourite places to work.
- Working on the train: this is like some kind of magic. Get me on a long train journey and I will smash through my list like never before.
- Reverse psychology: I'm not proud of this one but if all else fails, I tell myself not to do the task. It doesn't always work, but I have it up my sleeve as a last resort.
- Email bankruptcy: I got this one from an old friend who worked in corporate and said their boss would just delete the emails in their inbox when they got overwhelming, in the belief that 'if it's important, they will follow up'. Honestly, this is gold – so many emails are just other people's emergencies. I have tried this a few times and it's never failed me yet.

Right, with those top level go-to strategies covered, let's dig in to some of the detail.

10 Failing to plan

How to make a plan and stick to it

> **Planning is a great idea in theory. In practice, my brain prefers a series of chaotic miracles.**

Look at any list of ADHD weaknesses and somewhere near the top you're guaranteed to see the P word: planning. It falls into the category of working memory and executive functioning skills and can present a huge challenge to anyone running a business with ADHD. We're surrounded by phrases like 'if you fail to plan, then you plan to fail', but the truth is, when you're working with a brain that is built for novelty and reward, the minutiae of a plan just doesn't do it for us. It feels too big, too detailed and with too many moving parts to hold in our head.

We're not imagining it either – there is a huge amount of research into this area:

- According to a 2011 study by Russell Barkley,[21] 80–90 per cent of adults with ADHD report consistent difficulties

with executive functions like planning, organising, prioritising and time management.
- In a 2015 study of adults with ADHD,[22] 87 per cent reported problems with initiating and completing plans, especially when tasks were long-term or multi-step.
- A large-scale analysis in 2005[23] gathered results that translated to a 74–80 per cent likelihood that a randomly selected neurotypical person would outperform a person with ADHD in planning and organisation tasks.
- The Weiss Functional Impairment Rating Scale[24] – a validated scale measuring functional impairment in 'life skills' domains (planning, organising, managing responsibilities) – shows that over 75 per cent of adults with ADHD score in the clinical impairment range.

All that is to say, you're not making it up. Your brain is predisposed to being not-good at planning or figuring out the next steps.

Just to prove you're not alone, I'll share this story with you. I invented Canva. No joke – a year before they launched, I invented it. I wanted to find a way to democratise marketing for business owners and had the idea for a platform that had all the assets you would need to create your marketing designs. I got so excited by it, I could see it so clearly and there was nothing like it on the market. Then I did nothing with it. Canva is now worth $26 billion.

See – it's not just you!

This isn't a personal failing, or something you should have paid more attention to in school – it's something that you're just not optimised for, and that in itself should feel like a big fat permission slip to stop beating yourself up about it.

Instead, I want to state my case for reframing the way we view planning because while the concept of planning can feel overwhelming, the actual plan isn't where we struggle. Like so many other things in life, because we are told over and over again that we struggle with something, we just kind of end up believing it and it becomes fact in our head. Then, whenever a plan is needed, we immediately tell ourselves that's not something we can do, and either make a self-deprecating comment or avoid it altogether until we just become *The One Who Doesn't Plan*.

It's a label we gladly give ourselves and teach others to give us.

However, by the end of this chapter, I'll have shown you that it's just not true. We are actually great planners – INCREDIBLE in fact. We've just got 'planning' wrong.

So, what's going on? The ADHD connection

There is a cycle we go through to arrive at the point where we decide we are bad planners.

Have an idea > visualise it clearly in our heads > create 'A Plan' > get overwhelmed > don't follow the plan > execute badly > lose trust in ourselves and in our ability > *Toss another hoop on the 'Bad Planner' post*

Sound familiar?

It doesn't take too many cycles of that before our self-trust is in the gutter and we decide we are bad planners. But think about the different steps in that process:

- Vision: create the big-picture plan (on a sticky note, in a digital document, in your notes app, on the back of a napkin).
- Operation: create the operational plan with details on next steps.
- Execution: make the next steps happen.

There's a big difference between the vision stages (which we excel at) and the execution stages (where we don't).

Let's agree that from now on, we aren't going to lump everything into the concept of planning, and we'll look at planning and execution as two separate tasks and two different sets of skills.

Let's look at the planning bit first.

PLANNING

- Idea generation: this is an area where our brain is usually overactive. Coming up with ideas is rarely the challenge for us in business – in fact, it's usually the fun bit.
- Visualisation: we are excellent at this bit – we can see it, feel it and almost taste the rewards.
- Framework planning: we're good at this bit – we can see the big picture and what or who needs to be involved.

And now, execution.

EXECUTION

- Detailed planning: this is where it becomes harder – not because we are 'bad planners' but because we have poor working memory, so holding all the steps is hard.
- Stakeholder engagement: communication can be exhausting and again, due to working memory issues in our brain, it's hard to manage all the moving parts.
- Execution: the 'getting started' bit can feel like a physical barrier, especially if the dopamine has drained out of the project.
- Review and iteration: going back to a project once we have 'completed' it can feel really hard for our ADHD brain. We might feel there is no more dopamine to get from it, or RSD can kick in where we feel we might 'ruin' it or it won't be as good the second time.

So, execution is where we struggle and the root of our issues when it comes to this side of things is how our brain is – or isn't – wired to support executive function, a set of mental processes that help with managing time, staying organised, remembering details and regulating our attention and emotions.

Think of executive function like your brain's project manager. It helps you:

- set goals
- prioritise tasks
- start tasks
- stay focused
- adjust when things change
- follow through to completion.

For our brains, as we know from Part II, this system tends to be underpowered or inconsistent, mainly because our dopamine and norepinephrine levels are lower. These neurotransmitters are key for motivation, attention and reward – otherwise known as the key elements for following (or executing) a plan. The lack of dopamine, added to the way we process time, makes this *almost impossible* for us.

That's right, it's not a personal weakness or a character flaw – no amount of 'trying harder' or telling your brain to 'just focus!' will change your need for dopamine or your lack of natural skill in this area.

What you do need to remember is that for the pure planning bit, you are *on fire*:

- You will come up with ideas that people with execution skills are in awe of.
- You can create a vision faster than they have opened a new spreadsheet and given it the correct name so they can easily find it again.
- Without your big-picture scribbles on a whiteboard or back of a napkin, they would have nothing to create the operational plan from.

But if you don't separate planning from execution and simply tell yourself you're a bad planner full stop, there's a risk that you won't lean into the bits you're good at – and your whole business will be the worse for it.

My Brain First journey: Best-laid plans

I told myself for years that I was a terrible planner, or rather, I believed others when they told me I was a terrible planner. I would spend hours and hours on plans, colour-coding spreadsheets, trying to create new ways of planning that would somehow magically flick a switch in my brain that would mean I could actually go back and look at it once it was finished. But nothing worked, so I resigned myself to being the Bad Planner.

Then one day, I heard a story on the news that changed my perspective entirely. It was the story of the NASA Mars Climate Orbiter.[25] In December 1998, NASA launched the Mars Climate Orbiter, a space probe that was built at a cost of $125 million with the goal of studying the atmosphere, climate and surface changes on Mars.

This was a huge project for NASA and they had two separate teams working on it: a team responsible for building the craft and a team responsible for the navigation operations. But in September 1999, after ten months of travelling to Mars (no, that's not the shocking bit!), the orbiter combusted – burnt up and broke into pieces.

The celebrations on the ground quickly turned to shock, before an investigation began. It didn't take them long to work out what had happened: when working out vital acceleration data to understand HOW they got the craft to Mars, the navigation team provided their numbers using the metric system of millimetres, centimetres and metres, while the build team used the imperial system of inches, feet and pounds.

A project that two teams of best-in-class industry talent had worked on for years, at a cost of $125 million, had failed spectacularly because of a simple human communication error. It immediately made me feel better about the printed menus I designed with a very obvious typo on the cover of all 3,000 copies.

I think about the orbiter story a lot and every time it reminds me that there's a difference between planning and execution – and that even the best of us can get the execution side of things wrong.

Your Brain First business: Strategies for successful planning

If planning has become one of your freeze triggers, try adding these strategies to your Brain First Toolkit. We'll start with how to reframe your 'big-picture' thinking about planning and then move on to some specific tactics to help you with the day-to-day.

1. CHANGING YOUR PLANNING MINDSET

SEIZE THE MOMENT

Don't try to plan when you're already overwhelmed or distracted. Seize the moment when a moment of clarity hits and get your ideas down ... anywhere!

Remember, there is no one way to plan. Trust your own way of planning. Most of us are visual planners, so if that's you, try:

- sticky notes on a wall or whiteboard – try setting a timer for extra dopamine

- an old-school flipchart and literally drawing out your plan. It only has to make sense to you right now
- tools like Trello, Notion or Miro for visual mapping and use novelty to get a little boost.

PLAN IN PHASES

Don't overwhelm yourself with trying to look at the execution part yet, just focus on the zoomed-out roadmap and try viewing it in phases. So, if you were planning out your idea of introducing your product or service into new markets, it might look like:

- Phase 1 – Research
  - Understand size of opportunity
  - Research competitors
  - Look into customer demand
- Phase 2 – Operations
  - Who do I need support from?
  - What do I need them to do?
  - How will I promote the product/service?
- Phase 3 – Execution
  - Make it happen (with support)!

THINK ABOUT THE OPPORTUNITY COST

If you've figured out it's the execution side that you need help with but are telling yourself that it's ok for those who have support and you just can't afford it, try reframing that as whether you can afford *not to*. A good assistant or business manager is worth their weight in gold and can support with anything from managing your emails to making your plans happen.

Let's do some ADHD maths. Say you have an idea to introduce your product or service to a new market. You've done the sticky note numbers and can see this could add an extra 50,000–100,000 a year to your sales, but the initial excitement wears off once you start thinking about the steps it takes to actually make it happen. Here are your options: you don't do it and carry on as you are (for ever?) or you pay an assistant £20–40 an hour to work on the plan with you:

- They research the market.
- They understand the legal/financial implications of trading in the chosen new market.
- They look at the business case for expanding into the new market.
- They put together a plan to make it happen.
- They get your sign-off.
- They go and make it happen.

You have paid them maybe £1,500–2,500 to grow your sales by up to £100,000 a year. That is opportunity cost – the cost of not taking an opportunity: in this case, not bringing in the support you need for the work you need help with. It happens to the best of us.

2. TIPS AND ADVICE FOR IMPROVING DAY-TO-DAY PLANNING

REVERSE ENGINEER

Instead of relying on your working memory each day and trusting it to know what to do, set your vision for the week on a Monday by asking: 'What needs to be true by Friday?' Then map it backwards to figure out which tasks actually matter this week.

REPEAT WHAT WORKS (AND SCRAP WHAT DOESN'T)

Don't keep forcing planning tools that feel clunky or overwhelming. Test small tweaks each week:

- Plan in the morning vs planning in the evening.
- Using digital tools vs writing on paper.
- Plan for the day vs planning for the week.

Then keep what feels light and drop what doesn't – give yourself the permission to be ok with whatever works for you.

BUILD IN BODY DOUBLING OR CO-WORKING

Deliberately employ tactics to make the plan happen. Try:

- searching groups for in-person or virtual co-working sessions
- sharing your plan publicly or with a peer
- voice-noting your intentions to yourself for the day
- dumping them into AI for a helpful breakdown of how to tackle them and some encouragement.

PLAN FOR CHAOS

Whatever you're working on, the one thing that is guaranteed is disruption. Expect chaos (and be ok with it) by:

- adding in buffer zones by overestimating how long something will take
- using overflow hours in your calendar
- keeping Friday as a free day to wrap up or recover
- keeping 'chaos wildcard' days for when your brain just isn't playing – try not to force it every time.

KEEP IT VISIBLE

You know as well as I do that out of sight equals out of mind. Keep your plans where you can see them:

- a whiteboard in your workspace
- a screensaver with your weekly goals
- a sticky note dashboard on your desk.

Reframing what you thought you knew

Repeat after me: there is value in the time you spend planning – the hours you spend colour-coding, adding emojis and jumping between docs and spreadsheets trying to make something stick – even if the value is just getting it out of your head.

TL;DR

Planning isn't one thing done one way, it's a set of processes – some you are brilliant at, some not so good – done in any way that works for you.

11

Now, not now

Time management

> **ADHD time is either 'urgent panic' or 'I thought I had all day' ... there is no middle ground.**

The old trope about ADHD people being late for everything exists because it's true and it links to other clichés about ADHD: that we're forgetful and miss details. Forgetting appointments, not replying to emails or texts, or losing track of commitments are common for all of us – even with reminders in place, sticky notes all over the house and, of course, the new journal to help you keep track. Our working memory just isn't able to hold the details and this can be a real challenge in business – for us and for those around us.

None of these challenges stems from us not caring, or being lazy, or because we'd rather be sitting on our bed in a towel staring into space (although there is something uniquely wonderful about that specific experience!). It's because we process time differently – we don't see a linear timeline going left to right. Rather, some of us will visualise it going up and down, some as a whole and some of us aren't able to visualise it at all.

This is known as time blindness and can look like:

- hyperfocusing on low-priority tasks that feel urgent or exciting in the moment
- procrastinating, even over things you want to do, because they're not 'now'
- struggling with long-term planning as future consequences don't register because the future isn't 'real' yet (unless they are tied to strong emotions like excitement/shame/fear)
- things only becoming real when it's too late, e.g. ignoring a task until the deadline, then crashing into burnout trying.

Time blindness is a huge issue for many of us, but in business terms, the most challenging of these experiences are those related to *time collapse*.

Picture the scene: you've had your coffee, you've been for your walk and you're feeling good about the day ahead. But then you sit at your desk and see your (perfectly manageable) to-do list and have a complete meltdown – you go list-blind and dysphoric as you try to work out what to do first.

You're experiencing time collapse.

Time collapse happens because we struggle to prioritise our tasks based on urgency or importance, meaning that everything needs to be done right now.

I'm pretty sure you have, but if you haven't experienced it, it really is a horrible, panic-filled sensation where it feels impossible to take any kind of action.

So, what's going on? The ADHD connection

Time management is a huge struggle for people with ADHD and it impacts much more than being late for a coffee with friends. It's linked to the challenges with executive dysfunction that we have already looked at – the same set of brain functions responsible for planning, prioritising and organising.

Rather than processing time as a structured timeline of past – present – future, we tend to experience time as now/not now, i.e. it's either happening right now or it's happening 'not now' (which may as well mean it's not happening at all). This way of thinking can cause real problems in business.

The ADHD brain has a weak internal clock (linked to executive function), making it hard to plan, pace or prioritise effectively. This can show up as time passing much faster or slower than we thought, so deadlines creep up on us and tasks that 'won't take long' end up consuming a whole day.

In businesses where we plan projects or time-based sprints, time blindness and time collapse can manifest as a challenge with breaking down tasks and sequencing them, which means we veer between underestimating the time and effort required to complete a job and planning three days' worth of work into one. This leads to scope creep as you haven't been clear on the task deliverables, escalating costs as you throw money at solving the problem, and low self-esteem as you berate yourself for not completing the work in the time allocated.

Time management with ADHD isn't about managing time – it's about managing attention, energy and urgency perception. ADHD brains don't *feel* time the way neurotypical brains do. It's not about laziness or poor discipline. It's about navigating a brain that works in 'now' or 'not now'.

My Brain First journey: Our relationship with time

Growing up, I was late for everything.

My very well-meaning but horrifically late-for-everything dad was the main taxi service, which meant I built up huge anxiety around time keeping. I would be late for school events and friends' parties. I even missed the last train halfway back up the country after a visit home once, meaning I couldn't make it into work the next day and nearly lost my job.

Because of these experiences, I have a very uneasy relationship with time and constantly check my phone to know what time it is, what I should be doing, how long I have left, etc. My school bus left the village at 8.12 am and for years I thought I had some kind of magical gift because I would so often look at my phone and it was 8.12 am. Then I realised it was just because I was looking at my phone almost every minute of every day. Doing that, of course I saw 8.12 am (along with almost all other times on the clock).

My point is, this stuff is so layered, and if we have had experiences with being late to the point where it's caused us embarrassment or shame, that will impact how we relate to time as adults. When you pair that with the way our ADHD brain processes time anyway, you start to understand why you struggle.

This has impacted me in so many ways through my life and I am always early for everything now – and not like polite early, like weirdly 'erm, why are you here?' early. It drives my husband crazy and means I spend half my life waiting – not fun!

But I have one awful memory of when my time perception and (at that point) undiagnosed ADHD really did a number on me: it was the very early 2000s, I'd been to Barcelona for a few days with my then partner, and on the way home created the perfect ADHD storm. We got to the airport about four hours early so had a load of time to kill. I was in my safety zone – feeling calm and in control. For some reason – and do not ask me why – I had a watch on one wrist with the UK time and a watch on the other wrist with Spanish time. To cut a long story short, and I'm sure you're there already, we ended up missing our flight.

I can still feel the sense of panic and confusion when I realised that I had muddled the times and the plane had left without us. I was in total meltdown and nothing made sense. That was the first real panic attack I'd ever had and it changed the way I travel for ever – I am still stupidly early for all my flights, but I make sure I know exactly when I need to be at the gate ... and that I'm working to local time.

Your Brain First business: Bossing time management

If you struggle with time management in your business, give these strategies a go and add the ones that work for you into your Brain First Toolkit.

TIME AWARENESS OVER TIME MANAGEMENT

Time blindness isn't about scheduling, it's about visibility – you need to make sure you can literally see what time you have available for tasks. Get the basics right by overcompensating and surrounding yourself with visual aids. Try:

- setting visual timers so you don't lose track of time
- getting wall clocks in every room and making sure you wear a watch
- using your phone for alarms – I have them set for everything as a reminder.

PLANNING TIME BY ENERGY, NOT HOURS

Forget a 9–5 day, figure out your own energy patterns and work with that. If you are someone who has more energy in the mornings, then save that time for deep-focus tasks; if you come alive at 8 pm, then build your day around that. Time isn't set in stone – make it work for you. Try tracking your energy for a week, then building out your schedule from there.

TASK CALENDAR > TASK LIST

Have you ever noticed how hard the weekends and holidays can feel? That's because unstructured time is ADHD *hell*. In a work context, this means looking at a to-do list and then at a calendar featuring a range of different appointments doesn't always work for us. I recommend allocating time in your calendar not just to meetings but also to specific tasks. I find this works really well to calm my nervous system and show that I have plenty of time to get the work done – even if I don't end up sticking to it exactly. It might look like this:

- 10:00–11:00: Client meeting
- 11:15–11:45: Create five concepts for launch content
- 11:45–12:30: Respond to emails

BUILD TASK HABITS

Building task habits can be very beneficial to us. Think about the way you go to the kitchen and automatically open the fridge, or get into your car and reach for your phone to put on a podcast. We want to create those instinctive behaviours but for business. This can take time, but stick with it because it can make starting a task – and therefore sticking to your timings – so much easier. Try:

- 'When I finish my coffee, I open my laptop.'
- 'I light a candle, then I start my deep-focus work time block.'
- 'I put on my favourite podcast and then I create content.'

SET MICRO DEADLINES

Your urgency might only kick in as the actual deadline is looming – and that might be too late. Instead of risking it and stressing yourself out in the process, add in micro deadlines along the way. For example, I would always break down a client project into phases and then give each phase a micro deadline:

- Complete phase 1 in 3 weeks
- Complete phase 2 in 5 weeks
- Complete phase 3 in 3 weeks

This gives me something to work to and to share with the client for accountability. If you really struggle with this, you could try adding a reward to each milestone.

STOP TIME-FILLING

ADHD time management often falls apart when we over-schedule because we aren't able to forecast time. Try doing this to avoid over-filling your week:

- Always add in buffer blocks in case things overrun, to avoid pinch points.
- Remember you need time to recover – especially after high-output work.
- Protect one unstructured day per week to catch up and wrap up.

PLAN FOR YOUR BRAIN

Plan in 'now and not now' lists. When I first understood the concept of 'now and not now', it blew my mind because it made so much sense of my life! I created a Notion tool based on Now and Not Now planning and sold over 200 of them. Try breaking your list into now and not now tasks – or go to my website and grab a free copy of the ADHD Task Wizard.

REVIEW AND REBUILD WEEKLY

Treat yourself like the CEO that you are and review your week by asking:

- What went well in my time management?
- What threw me off and disrupted my plan?
- What do I want to keep next week?
- What do I want to change next week?

Reframing what you thought you knew

Your brain is predisposed to being bad at time management, but that doesn't mean you have to be the 'late friend' for ever.

Understanding the pinch points in your life will help you build better systems around them.

TL;DR

Your brain processes time differently from a neurotypical brain.

Time blindness and time collapse can impact your business on many levels, so building your Brain First business around your experience of them is key.

12

The scroll hole

Why procrastination isn't the problem

> ADHD means I won't start until it's urgent, but I've learnt to trust myself that it will get done, so it's ok.

Of all the ways ADHD impacts our businesses there is one culprit that gets the blame far more than any other. In fact, if I asked you what the biggest barrier to growing your business is, I can guarantee at least 90 per cent of you would tell me it's procrastination. Right?

Well, I'm happy to tell you that you're wrong.

The dictionary definition of procrastination is the 'action of *delaying* or *postponing* something'.[26] But I think it's actually come to mean something slightly different. When we talk about procrastinating, we're not talking about the act of putting off a task, we're usually talking about what we spend that time doing.

Let's look at a normal day in your business. You're feeling good, you know what you need to do and you're confident you can comfortably fit it into the working calendar. You sit down at your desk and, remembering some business advice you once read, you decide to 'eat the frog' and get the worst jobs out of the way first. (If you've never read the book the phrase 'eat the frog' comes from, please don't – it's a great book but it's terrible advice for ADHD brains, for all the reasons I am about to dive into.) Looking at your list, the perfect frog jumps out at you: 'complete spreadsheet for accountant'.

In fact, you don't even have to look to know that's your frog because it's been staring at you for weeks now as you move it from list to list, feeling that dread in the pit of your stomach every time you see it staring back at you.

So today is the day, you're finally going to do it. And so you open up the spreadsheet, take a deep breath and get ready to ... oooh, lemme check Instagram!

You get to 11 am and realise that not only did you *not* complete the spreadsheet (for the fourth day in a row) but you now feel even worse because you've seen that one of your Instagram friends has won an award for their business, another one is on a weekend break to New York with some clients and someone you've never met but works in the same fields as you has just done a Ted Talk on the topic you always said *you* wanted to do a Ted Talk on.

Cue toddler tantrum

So, what's going on? The ADHD connection

Now for the science(-ish) bit. As you'll recall from Chapter 1, and as we've been exploring throughout the book, ADHD brains are motivated by only two things: interest and excitement. More specifically, this breaks down into INCU:

- Interest
- Novelty
- Competition
- Urgency

If you are trying to make your brain do a task that doesn't tick one of those boxes, you don't stand a single chance of getting that done. This is literally the definition of working against your brain.

The more you try, the more you will feel resistance to it. Cue 'procrastination'. You pick up your phone, you go to the fridge, you have a cigarette, and *that* is your trigger for frustration, shame and judgement.

We will often beat ourselves up for leaving things until the last minute. Whether it's preparing a slide deck for work or buying a birthday card for a friend, you can guarantee if it's happening on the Friday, you'll find me doing it on the Thursday night.

I LIVE in the last minute, seriously, I do! And I am more than ok with it because do you know when my life got infinitely easier? When I *accepted* that my brain needs urgency to function and I stopped blocking out hours and hours in my calendar to do the task the week before, only to move it, then move it again, then move it again, each time berating myself furiously.

Now I save myself all that drama by just adding it in the day before or the morning it's needed. I know it will be done and I won't have to have gone through all that torture leading up to it.

The fact is, if you work with your brain and allow it to do the jobs it wants to do, that excite it and appeal to interest and novelty, everything will become urgent in the end anyway. The thing will always get done.

That is truly Brain First thinking.

My Brain First journey: All the times we don't do the thing

I once worked with a client, let's call her Sarah (not her real name). She told me procrastination was the reason she was scared of starting her business and that it was the biggest issue her ADHD presented. The more we dug into how this manifested for her, the more we realised that the issue wasn't procrastination at all.

The conversation we had is one I go back to a lot because it was so transformative to watch it play out in real time. She was basically saying, 'I don't want to start this business because I can't focus for eight hours like I *should* be able to.'

I asked her to explain exactly what happens when she procrastinates. She told me that she sits down to do some work and then the next thing she knows, she is scrolling dating apps and an hour or more has gone by. Because of some experiences she'd had, using these apps brought with it a feeling of shame and judgement which could impact her so much that the rest of the day was a write-off. I asked her when this happened, trying to understand the trigger for her to start scrolling. After some discussion, we identified the common thread was the jobs that she just *didn't want to do*.

You might be thinking, well yeah, of course they are. But how often have you recognised a chain of events like this in your own life:

- You try to do a task you don't 'want' to do (I'll come back to this).
- You find a distraction like scrolling/sticking your head in the fridge/going for a cigarette.
- You realise you still haven't done the task and beat yourself up for it.
- You go back to your distraction method.
- Cycle repeats.

The conclusion for us both was that procrastination is a two-part curse: the task that triggers it AND the distraction method you revert to.

Your Brain First business: Crushing procrastination

If you struggle with procrastination in your business, here are some of my go-to strategies. Try them out and pop the ones that work for you in your Brain First Toolkit.

NO BIG TASKS

If your to-do list is full of big, vague tasks (I know mine is) then your brain will HATE it. Break them down, break them down and break them down again.

So often we list goals instead of tasks, so first of all check that you're actually working with a task, not a goal. For example: write copy for 'About' page on website (task); redo website (goal).

Then break the task down into the smallest steps that you can so you only have tickable tasks on your list. Instead of 'create email funnel', you would have:

- create flow framework in email platform
- map out email parts
- write headline, purpose and call to action (CTA) for each email
- write emails
- check links
- launch funnel.

Breaking everything down like this helps to maintain your interest – crossing off those manageable little steps will give you the dopamine hit you need to get through the job at hand.

GAMIFY THE FIRST STEP

Gamifying your productivity is such a hack – I use this all the time in my business. Give these a go:

- Estimate the time it will take you to complete a task, then set a timer and try to beat the time you've allocated.
- Reward yourself with ten minutes of guilt-free scrolling once you've completed the task.
- Set a timer and see how many tasks you can tick off in ten minutes.

Here you're competing with yourself, or the clock, and that jolt of extra energy will keep you hooked in for longer.

TIMEBOX

Timeboxing is a great way to get started. Tell yourself if you get 30 minutes' work done, then that is enough. Once you get started, you will more than likely carry on because you have removed the pressure and perfectionism that were causing you to procrastinate in the first place; it also taps into your love of urgency. That time limit is telling your brain to kick into gear before the clock runs out.

MAKE IT MATTER

Instead of berating yourself or trying to bully your brain into getting to work by guilting it, try linking the task to your goals or results and make it matter *to you*, not just to your to-do list. Instead of 'I *should* send this email', try 'sending this gets me closer to hiring help and feeling less overwhelmed'. There's an interest angle here – you'll be more motivated when you focus on the outcome that gets you closer to your overall aims than on the more mundane task that's sitting on the desk.

USE A 'NEXT ACTION' COLUMN

I love this one and use it all the time in my business. Rather than overwhelming projects or task lists that we know won't get done, keep a 'next action' column so you only have one thing to tick off. Again, this is about creating interest and the little dopamine boosts you need to get through chunky work.

Project	**Next action**
Podcast	Write three episode titles
Launch	Write five concepts for launch content
Client work	Respond to Sarah's email

INTERRUPT THE SPIRAL

Did you ever hear the saying 'a change is as good as a rest'? Well, that's true with procrastination, too. If you're frozen, change physical and emotional state with these:

- Move your body (walk, stretch, jump).
- Get some fresh air.
- Change room or location.
- Play a song and dance it out.
- Go and work from a coffee shop or library.

This is definitely in the 'novelty' category of INCU. Surprise your body and mind with a change and it might just surprise you right back.

EMBRACE SCRAPPINESS

Perfectionism is just procrastination in disguise. Get it done and sent – done is always better than perfect. Action breeds clarity, not the other way round, so fight perfectionism with scrappy action next time it rears its perfect but very ugly head:

- Write a rubbish first draft.
- Launch before it's 'ready'.
- Jump and learn how to fly on the way down.

Here you're mixing interest and novelty with a bit of urgency – sometimes an injection of fear can be just the springboard we need.

Reframing what you thought you knew

You aren't lazy, you have been working against your brain and trying to force it to do tasks it can't do, triggering your procrastination spiral.

Imagine you have a friend who is allergic to animals. You plan a day out and excitedly tell them you're going to the zoo. They remind you of their allergies and say they would rather not go, but you ignore them and bundle them onto the train, push them through the zoo gates and drag them around the enclosures, pointing out all the animals along the way, expecting them to be excited.

Kinda ridiculous, right?

This isn't about us letting our brain run the show (please God, don't do that!), but it is about avoiding putting it in a place of struggle. Life can feel hard enough as it is; the last thing we need is to spend any more time at war with ourselves. Understanding what we need to do to reach our goals, and working with our brain to get it done, will get us where we want to be without the pain (or any awkward zoo excursions).

Procrastination happens when you create conflict with your brain. If it isn't interested or excited by the task, it will find the dopamine elsewhere.

TL;DR

Your brain is only motivated by interest, novelty, competition or urgency, so making it do a task that doesn't fall into those categories is pointless. Try focusing on the tasks that interest or excite you and watch how that impacts your procrastination.

13

Cognitive quicksand

Context switching

> **Multitasking sounds productive, but for ADHD brains it often leaves a trail of half-finished tasks in our wake, which means we start each day already overwhelmed.**

ADHD is full of contradictions and none more so than the fact it delivers us a brain that needs variety and craves change but struggles with task switching and the transitions that need to happen in between. Context switching is the process of shifting your attention between tasks, environments or mental frameworks, e.g. jumping from writing an email to taking a call and then prepping for a meeting.

This is a huge problem when we're running our own businesses and every day is like a different task from *The Apprentice*, with a million sub-tasks to complete.

In a famous 2008 study, 'The cost of interrupted work: More speed and stress' by Gloria Mark,[27] 48 participants acted as HR managers responding to emails while being interrupted by phone or instant messenger to test how different types of interruptions affected speed, stress and performance. The findings were fascinating (and keep in mind that the study didn't screen for neurodivergence, so these results are across all brains).

- Both same-context and different-context interruptions had similar effects. In other words, if you were interrupted writing an email by another email popping in, it would have the same effect as if you were writing an email and someone came to ask you a question.
- Participants worked faster and wrote shorter emails when interrupted, completing tasks on average two minutes faster than in uninterrupted conditions. However, this speed came at the cost of higher mental workload, stress, frustration, time pressure and effort.
- Individuals scoring higher on pre-test checks around 'Openness to Experience' and 'Need for Personal Structure' handled interruptions more efficiently, reporting shorter task times.

In a follow-up interview with Fast Company,[28] Mark revealed that they found 'it takes an average of 23 minutes and 15 seconds to get back to the task'.

Twenty-three minutes to refocus? And that was based on a cross-section of brains.

Neurodivergent brains are at a distinct disadvantage when it comes to context switching due to our inability to focus and difficulty when it comes to completing transitions – and the impact this is almost definitely having on your business is significant.

You will be all too familiar with this yourself, I'm sure: that feeling when you've finally found your groove with a task you've been putting off for days, then an email pings in, someone asks you a question or your phone rings and *POOF*, the focus is gone and the ability to get back into it just feels too far out of reach.

So, what's going on? The ADHD connection

Context switching is *brutal* for ADHD brains. Every time you jump from one task or focus area to another, your brain has to reboot. It costs energy, attention and time – and it creates a backlog of open loops that can leave you feeling scattered and unproductive.

Context switching isn't easy for anyone, but neurodivergent brains tend to experience it as a much more energy-draining, emotionally loaded and disruptive process. It's not just annoying, it can derail an entire day.

Looking at some of the specifics of context switching we can see how many aspects fit into areas of the ADHD experience that we've already looked at and identified as challenging.

COGNITIVE LOAD SWITCHING

This is the toll it actually takes on your brain to stop one task and start another – the same way a car uses more fuel from a cold start, our brain needs more energy to get going too. While a neurotypical brain might find the actual process of switching from one task to another takes effort, it is more easily manageable, whereas the toll on a neurodivergent brain is high, with each switch feeling exhausting and overwhelming.

TASK RE-ENGAGEMENT

A neurotypical person can return to their task and find focus with relative ease, while a neurodivergent brain can struggle to re-engage or refind the dopamine and motivation it needs to get going again after it has been distracted.

WORKING MEMORY

A neurotypical brain has a more consistent working memory and is able to hold the steps of a task while switching. A neurodivergent brain has poor working memory which will 'drop' mid-switch, resulting in the feeling of having to start again.

EXECUTIVE FUNCTION

We know this is a huge challenge for neurodivergent brains, impacting initiating or stopping tasks by adding in friction points. A neurotypical brain is generally more stable and finds planning, prioritising and moving through tasks much easier.

SENSORY LOAD

Neurodivergent brains can find stress is amplified by environmental triggers such as smells, sounds or visual clutter, which impacts the way we handle task switching, whereas neurotypical brains generally find it easier to filter out background noises and distractions so they can focus on the task in front of them.

EMOTIONAL REGULATION

Neurotypical brains can be more resilient and handle interruptions as part of the process. Neurodivergent brains are more prone to emotional dysregulation during interruptions or shifts, which impacts the way we handle the transition.

FLOW STATE

The state we find ourselves in when we are mid-task and really in our flow is much easier to exit and then re-enter for a neurotypical brain, but our brain can find breaking hyperfocus physically and emotionally painful (which is just another thing that sounds ridiculous to someone who doesn't experience it).

My Brain First journey: Themed days

My Brain First business now looks like a few different services and revenue streams that keep me interested and give my brain variety, which I love. The problem comes when I am focused on one of them but get pulled into a task for another by a rogue notification or a too-good-to-ignore idea. When that happens, this piece of advice I heard years ago has, largely, saved me.

I heard Sara Blakely, the ADHD founder of Spanx, speaking and she acknowledged that the biggest challenge to her productivity while growing her company was context switching – and the biggest change came when she began giving each day a theme.

She gave the example of how, before she started to set themes, she would be working on something important to do with finance, when someone would come and ask her to sign off a colour scheme for an exhibition and she'd give it the ok. Then she would see it in real life and wonder how they got it so wrong, only to be told that she had actually signed it off herself.

She realised that context switching was no good for her ADHD brain – she simply couldn't meaningfully move quickly from one task to another – so she started theming her days into marketing, product, future planning, etc instead.

I started doing this after hearing about it and it was a real game changer. While it doesn't solve every problem every time, it definitely helps and now I actually go one step further and break my week into 'input' and 'output' days. This marks a difference between a day I am focused on my business (input) or on delivery (output), and that really helps me to set boundaries around the access other people have to me and my time.

This needs to be implemented with some thought, care and communication – you can't just decide you aren't going to respond to clients on a Monday and Friday and then begin! I would start by allocating the days, then deciding how to communicate that to the affected parties, and updating booking software, contracts, etc.

For example, I like to have an email autoresponder to set out expectations, so if a client emails me on a Monday, I know that they know I'm not available and they will hear from me on Tuesday. This means I'm not flicking between my task and my inbox and there is no room for miscommunication. This is how mine looks:

Monday = (input) Marketing: content/business development/creative
Tuesday = (input) Projects/new ideas
Wednesday = (output) Clients/programmes/meetings
Thursday = (output) Clients/programmes/meetings
Friday = Free day

Your Brain First business: Strategies for successful task-switching

If context switching is a struggle for you, give these strategies a go and add whichever work for you to your Brain First Toolkit.

BATCHING AND BLOCKING

Your brain performs best when it can stay in one 'mode' at a time: writing mode, admin mode, people mode, etc. Grouping tasks means fewer mental transitions, which ultimately means more focus. For example:

- Writing: content, email newsletter and copy.
- Admin: finance, inbox management and reports.
- Offline: in-person meetings, events.

Don't forget that batching tasks also means blocking out others – when you're focusing on one of these, don't let other jobs creep in. Don't forget that you can also extend this to full days, as I described before. So, for example:

Monday = content
Tuesday = projects
Wednesday = calls
Thursday = client delivery
Friday = overflow/catch-up

USE TIME ANCHORS

Structure your day with specific but generous and flexible time blocks. This reduces the need to jump between tasks without ever getting deep into any of them because you know you have time allocated for it later in the day. For example:

10:00–12:00: content block
13:00–14:00: email and admin
14:00–16:00: client work

PRE-DECIDE THE NEXT TASK

At the end of each time block, jot down what you're going to do next. This reduces that in-between fog where you're staring at your screen thinking, 'What now?'

PLAN FOR RECOVERY TIME

Switching focus takes more than just attention, it drains your nervous system and leaves you fatigued. Add in 5–15-minute recovery blocks between context shifts to reset your cognitive load.

Here are a few ideas to try:

- Stretch or move.
- Get fresh air.
- Try some simple breathing exercises.
- Zone out – stare out of the window.
- Do a 'nothing' task like cleaning.

LIMIT YOUR TABS

Too many browser tabs or open projects lead to mental fragmentation. Try these to limit the number of browser tabs you have open at once:

- Use tools like OneTab or Google Chrome's 'group' feature to manage browser tabs.
- Avoid diving straight into the browser rabbit hole by having only one browser window open per focus area (for example, one for writing, one for email).

HELP YOUR BRAIN STORE IDEAS FOR THE FUTURE

Stave off the desire to jump on ideas the moment they occur by creating easy ways to put them to one side (and not lose them) while you finish the task in hand:

- Keep a 'parked ideas' list for thoughts that pop up mid-task.
- When something comes up, ask Siri to remind you about it in 10/30 minutes (whenever you anticipate finishing the task).

CREATE A TRANSITION TOOL

When you do decide it's time to transition between jobs, or you're interrupted and don't have a choice to put the new activity on hold, use this strategy to help you offload the open loop so your brain doesn't try to juggle the task you were doing and the thing you're stopping it to do. Before switching tasks, stop and write down:

- what you were just doing
- what you were going to do next (so you can do it when you return to the task)
- what needs to happen to complete the task.

REDUCE HAT-SWITCHING

If you're a solo business owner, you might be the CEO, marketer, coach, admin assistant and IT person in one day. That's too much for anyone, especially when you have ADHD.

Try limiting the amount of hat-switching, which adds further brain load to context switching:

- Outsource low-value roles to an assistant.
- Limit hat-switching to 1–2 per day.
- Use 'hat hours' (e.g. 9–11 am = CEO time).

Reframing what you thought you knew

Sure, context switching isn't our best suit, but recognising the power of hyperfocus and building our daily structure with that in mind is key.

You will never be able to focus for eight hours straight, switching hats all day long – you will burn out. But there will be a way for YOU to manage all the tasks you need to manage in the time you have available.

TL;DR

Context switching is something you do every day that drains your battery and adds to your burnout cycle – and it's a tricky one to tackle because our brain craves the novelty and variety that switching gives us.

The key is to find a way to retain the novelty but reduce the unnecessary switches that mean we are doing 50 per cent of everything and leaving a trail of unfinished tasks in our wake.

14

Why does everything feel so hard now?

Skill regression

> **Skill regression often means your capacity for masking has changed, not your capability for the skill in question. It's important to know the difference.**

There is a unique phenomenon we experience post-ADHD diagnosis or identification, and that is the feeling of skill regression. Tasks or activities that once felt easy suddenly feel difficult or even impossible. It's a really confusing experience, and one that can feel isolating, because how do you explain to someone that you can no longer sit in that meeting or update that spreadsheet or go to that event?

As with all these things, I find that having the words to explain and understand what is going on makes a huge difference to how you experience it. So let me set out the truth: you were never a natural at sitting in that meeting or updating that spreadsheet or going to that event – I mean, you *could*, but it was the reason you then went home and emptied a bottle of wine, spent all evening watching brain-rot TV or didn't want to see anyone at the weekend. But what's happened now is that you are unmasking.

If you have spent any time at all consuming ADHD content, you will have come across the term 'masking' – hiding or concealing your neurodivergent traits to appear more neurotypical – and its opposite, unmasking – getting comfortable with being entirely yourself, accepting your brain the way it is.

When you unmask, whether it's something that you're doing consciously or unconsciously, skill regression can be a consequence.

Sometimes this is because you feel more able to show people the 'real' you, the one that truly does hate long agendas and endless minutes, and so you can begin to deliberately step back from the jobs that drain you. You are giving yourself permission not to be 'good' at things you struggle with.

But sometimes (and this is when it can feel more unsettling) it's not a deliberate choice – it's as though, as your energy level for masking and pretending to like and be good at certain tasks starts to slip, so does your ability to actually complete the tasks themselves.

So, what's going on? The ADHD connection

Unmasking, whether it's deliberate or not, leaves you feeling vulnerable. It feels as risky and uncertain as pulling at a thread of a jumper you've spent your whole life knitting, not knowing which bits will unravel, which will stay intact and what, exactly, you'll be left with.

Surely it's just easier to carry on wearing the jumper the way it is?

Well, with masking, you don't get to choose, unfortunately. The moment that you get the answer to your lifelong question about who you really are, and you start to process that it was never personal weaknesses or a character flaw but the way your brain is wired that makes you act the way you do, then you can finally take a big deep breath and let your shoulders drop. And skill regression can kick in.

As I said before, moments when you are suddenly honest about your capabilities are in some ways easier to manage than the loss of skills that takes you by surprise, but there are ways of managing both.

When you recognise that something you used to be able to cope with no longer feels achievable and you can link it to your ADHD, the work is around being honest with yourself and with those you trust to set up a new kind of normal.

Where a skill that you've relied on in the past suddenly evades you ... well, that's when some tips and tricks to help you manage the situation can become invaluable (and where the 'Your Brain First business' section will become your go-to).

My Brain First journey: Diagnosis and perimenopause

I have experienced a few stages of skill regression in my business journey, including once when I was first diagnosed and once when I hit perimenopause, and let me tell you, even though I talk, write and think about this stuff day in, day out, they hit me like a brick.

I have built multi-million-pound businesses, worked day and night through week- (if not month-) long periods of hyperfocus, and would absolutely pride myself on being able to do ANYTHING. Then my diagnosis came and at first it was less regression and more permission. It was an utter JOY to no longer have to pretend to fill out spreadsheets that seemed totally pointless. It was amazing to be able to put a 30-minute limit on meetings, and to understand – and help others understand – why I needed to do it.

But bit by bit, and ever so subtly, I started to see that I just wasn't able to push myself in the way that I used to.

If I was burnt out, I couldn't simply put on a smile and 'crack on with it'; if I couldn't instantly understand something, I really struggled to go to five different places to piece together the information; and the communication part of running a business with a growing team became almost impossible.

The next time I hit skill regression was even less fun: perimenopause. If you're a woman who has been through it, you will get it. If you're a woman who hasn't yet been through it, you need to know about it. And if you're a man who will never go through it, well, we would love for you to have enough of a sense of what's going on to be able to ally with the women around you.

Peri-menopause is the transitionary phase your hormones go through in the lead-up to menopause – and for women with ADHD this can be *brutal*. The average duration is four years, but it can last up to ten.[29]

Yes, TEN YEARS.

It is also an incredibly high-risk period for women with ADHD, which can trigger a significant worsening of symptoms and, where it was previously undiagnosed, reveal ADHD. Hormonal changes, especially oestrogen dropping, interact with neurotransmitters (dopamine, serotonin), affecting our brain performance around attention, memory and mood.

- In a sample of 3,117 women (aged 46+), 61 per cent said ADHD had the greatest impact on their daily lives between ages 40 and 59.[30]
- Within that group, 43 per cent were first diagnosed between ages 41 and 50, suggesting perimenopause is a key window for first diagnoses.
- About 73 per cent reported experiencing anxiety and 63 per cent reported depression.

But I entered all of this blindly. I'd heard of perimenopause, I'd heard women who were much older than me talk about it, and it definitely wasn't something I needed to think about ... until it was, and I knew NOTHING about it.

'We didn't have it in my day,' my mum said.

Yes, you did mum, there just wasn't a name for it.

Essentially for me it has become a period of existential crisis where I have questioned everything I have ever thought – and also forgotten how to spell my own name and called a locksmith to change my office locks only to find my keys in the fridge an hour later (true story).

The mix of perimenopausal skill regression (itself a combination of hormonal brain fog and the fact that our resources to mask are just stripped bare) and ADHD skill regression has been pretty potent. In a business sense, it has meant that on some days I will look at my list and feel really excited about a super-detailed task like planning or forecasting numbers, while another day I will look at it and physically want to run for the hills because I couldn't even tell you where I would start with it. I can feel all of those core skills come and go and it's very unsettling.

Never have I been more grateful to have built a business that had the flex and flow in it to deal with the level of unpredictability perimenopause has brought.

Of course, you might be wondering why I'm going into detail about this in an ADHD business book, but skill regression (which definitely impacts how we manage ourselves and our businesses) is something that many of us will face post-diagnosis, and for those who experience it with the double whammy of perimenopause, something we are still just not speaking about enough, it's truly shocking. Gathering some strategies to help you when skill regression hits is the best way forward – forewarned is forearmed, after all.

Your Brain First business: How to handle times of skill regression

NAME IT TO TAME IT

This is such a great tip for any ADHD trait, but especially useful for skill regression.

Say to yourself: 'This is skill regression, not failure.' When you internalise it as incompetence, the shame spiral kicks in. When you name it as a temporary state, you can problem-solve from compassion and self-acceptance.

CREATE MINI SOPs

When you're doing something you can do easily, record it and create standard operating procedures for your business.

Use screenshots, video walkthrough, voice notes or checklists so future-you can follow past-you's instructions when the skill is hard to access. This is particularly helpful for anything that's very routine or task-based (like the process for setting up a new client in the CRM).

BUILD A SECOND BRAIN

Think of your brain as for working memory only: you don't need to store everything in there. Create a second brain that holds all the information you need to access quickly and free your brain up for the fun stuff. Try using:

- tools like Notion (I LOVE Notion), Trello or Google Drive to store your daily SOPs
- AI to generate instructions on the fly – there are some tools available that will read your screen and build the process for you
- sticky notes/Post-its and notebooks on your desk for frequent tasks.

STICK TO MICRO TASKS

Rather than trying to complete the full task, start with the simplest version of the skill:

- Instead of 'write an email', try 'open the doc and write a sentence'.
- Instead of 'launch a full campaign', start with 'draft an Instagram caption'.

Yes, it might sound patronising, but treating yourself like a toddler is actually a great way to get through this.

REVISIT PAST-YOU

Go back to a previous piece of work you successfully completed in a similar area and take time to think about the process you followed. Even just seeing the work and reminding yourself it's a skill you used to have will help you to see that it's possible again. Ask yourself:

- 'What used to make this easy for me?'
- 'What might help me feel safe doing this again?'

Sometimes skill regression is a trauma response, so your brain might be associating the skill with pressure, risk or perfectionism.

NORMALISE THE CYCLE

ADHD isn't linear; we don't 'master' a skill for ever – we re-access it in cycles, so let go of the idea that consistency equals memory.

Instead, build systems that assume forgetfulness is part of the plan and be compassionate when it happens. The worst thing is to start telling ourselves stories about what it means when we are unable to do something.

Reframing what you thought you knew

Skill regression is your brain unmasking and showing you what it is capable of. Try to focus on all the things you do so well because the chances are that the areas you are regressing in are the areas that were actually burning you out.

TL;DR

Skill regression is a natural part of diagnosis or realisation.

You're not regressing – you're unmasking, and along with it losing the skills that were never suited to you.

15

I can take on the WORLD

Activating and managing God Mode

> **The key to managing God Mode is to make sure you're not writing cheques that your burnt-out self will have to cash.**

God Mode: that feeling that you can do anything and take over the world.

If you don't experience it, then think of it as HyperfocusPLUS. It has all the customary trademarks of hyperfocus but it can last much longer, with some people reporting it lasting days or even weeks. And whereas hyperfocus tends to be monotropic, i.e. you have deep focus on one thing, God Mode is broader and allows you to switch and take on new tasks. In fact, THE MORE NEW THINGS, THE BETTER!

Fun fact: when pulling together more research on God Mode for this book, I turned to Google and the very first hit was an

Instagram post I made in 2023 about my love/hate relationship with it. I have spoken about this topic extensively online and it can be pretty divisive, with people who don't experience it saying I'm not describing ADHD but a manic episode. And perhaps in some ways they are right, it does feel slightly manic (chaotic, even), but it can also be incredibly powerful.

When you're in God Mode, you want to bottle it, yet one of the most frustrating things about it is that it's elusive and impossible to replicate on demand, whereas hyperfocus happens when one of our core INCU triggers are at play:

- Interest
- Novelty
- Competition
- Urgency

God Mode doesn't follow the same pattern. I have tried tracking mine to hormones, environment, activity or other external factors, as yet with no success.

God Mode feels great because the day-to-day struggles we experience, like struggling to focus, lack of clarity and executive function, are like a distant memory as we smash through our tasks with little to no trouble.

So, what's going on? The ADHD connection

God Mode is your brain overcorrecting for dopamine deficiency, executive dysfunction and its constant need for urgency. And although it isn't an official term, it's a very real experience for many of us. Neuroscience can give us some explanation of what's happening under the bonnet, so let's take a look.

God Mode is an extreme form of hyperfocus, where attention locks in *too* tightly, often on something urgent, novel or deeply interesting. It's different from *flow*, which feels calm, controlled and sustainable – hyperfocus is intense, compulsive and often triggered by urgency or emotional drive.

I asked my community on Instagram what their experience of God Mode was and how it differs from hyperfocus. Here are some of their responses:

> Luuk: Unlimited inspiration and the ability to BURN through my to-do list.
> Leah: I actually get annoyed when I have to STOP working!
> Michael: When I'm in God Mode it's like some blissful dream. I don't have to think about a single movement.
> Jo: I always push it too far because it just feels so good, but little me is on my shoulder saying 'you know what comes next'.
> Becky: Invincible and confident – completing tasks without the three-day build-up. Like, I can just DO THE THING!

As I think more about these ideas, I realise just how different hyperfocus is from God Mode:

Hyperfocus is:

- task focused
- emotionally triggered
- somewhat easy to replicate
- short, sharp periods.

God Mode is:

- variety focused – the more tasks, the better!
- fleeting, elusive and unpredictable
- impossible to replicate
- extended periods of time.

Whereas hyperfocus is triggered by interest, novelty, competition or urgency, God Mode is less predictable and seems to be the product of a perfect storm:

- You have work that excites you and you're clear on.
- You are feeling mentally resilient.
- You're riding a dopamine wave, perhaps from some validation or recognition.

When God Mode is triggered, dopamine floods the system, giving you that rush of clarity and motivation. That spike kicks the brain into gear, overriding the usual executive function issues that would hold us back from getting started or completing a task.

During God Mode, your brain loses track of time and can also filter out distractions that would normally derail you from completing your work. That's why people often describe it as a 'superpower' because your brain is finally doing what it *knows* how to do but rarely gets to do.

Many of the people I work with LOVE a period of God Mode but have learnt to approach it with caution because over time, it can become exhausting and damaging – physically and emotionally. The very fact that it's so unpredictable is what makes it so hard to temper, because when it finally lands, it just feels SO GOOD to have the clarity, energy and motivation to get stuff done, in comparison with the usually daily battle.

But you really must, or the combination of dopamine flooding your system and cognitive over-exertion will almost certainly land you in burnout.

My Brain First journey: My relationship with God Mode

Before my ADHD diagnosis, I loved these periods of uber-productivity. I could do the work of ten people; I could smash through my to-do list and be hungry for more; I could say yes to every project, event or opportunity that came my way. I actually thought that was who I was – I would take on more and more because I backed myself, I knew I could handle it.

However, once I got my diagnosis and started to understand more about my brain, I realised what was happening was an extended period of hyperfocus that was almost guaranteed to land me in burnout, and so I started viewing it differently. Rather than milking the moment for all it was worth, I started to approach with caution. I would stop and ask myself if Burnout Me would be able to honour the commitment I was about to make, and it honestly changed the game.

Not only did I find that it would extend that period of God Mode – meaning I felt locked in and focused for longer – it also meant that the following period of burnout was less deep and

I wasn't left with a load of cheques to cash that God Mode Me had written.

Previously, I would look at a calendar week and see a load of events or commitments that were just way too much for anyone to manage, then trace them back to an episode of God Mode where I had agreed to them all. I then had the awful decision to make: do I let people down or do I overstretch myself?

One thing I know by now is that overstretching myself just isn't a great option. It always, always ends in tears and I just won't allow myself to do it these days, especially if travel and masking are involved. But back then, I would be left to cancel plans, often at the last minute, which is never a good thing.

You don't have to experience that too many times to realise something has to change, so now my God Mode is much more tempered because I know otherwise it is just a precursor to burnout.

Your Brain First business: How to make the most of God Mode

If you experience God Mode, then give these strategies a go to help you work with God Mode intentionally, not destructively.

RECOGNISE IT

You will likely be in the habit of celebrating when it hits, so this will take some practising, but as soon as you feel it kick in, stop and recognise that it's happening. This simple moment of mindfulness lets you direct the energy rather than getting swept away by it. 'Ok, we're in God Mode. How can I best use this energy so I don't burn out?'

PICK *ONE* THING

God Mode can trick you into thinking you can do everything at once. Resist the urge by asking yourself: 'If I only get one big thing done today, what would make the biggest difference to my business?' Be conscious about how you use your time and energy.

RESTRICT YOUR FOCUS

Build parameters for yourself and set up your day to manage your energy by splitting your time into working sprints and allowing for recovery in between. For example: 'I'll work in God Mode for 90 minutes, then I must take a break, eat or move my body.' Set alarms, use timers or get an accountability partner to keep you on track.

CREATE BACK-UP SPACE

God Mode will see you come up with even more ideas and side quests than usual – and if you act on them all, you will end up in a whole world of pain, with a million unfinished tasks for future-you to clear up.

To stop this happening, create a back-up space:

- Dump ideas into a Notion board or voice note.
- Ask Siri to remind you of your ideas later in the day.

- Create a God Mode folder for the random ideas that pop up.
- Leave yourself notes like 'This is a good idea, but not urgent'.

BUILD FOR BURNOUT

God Mode isn't sustainable, so treat it like an energy loan you'll need to repay sooner or later. If you know you're going into a sprint, pre-book the downtime. That means:

- cancel tomorrow's meetings
- plan for low-output tasks the next day
- build in a decompression buffer after the focus session
- always keep future-you in mind.

ACCEPT THAT YOU CAN'T FORCE IT

This state is unpredictable and you're either in it or you're not. Treat it like the exception, not the rule, and never try to force it when it's not there. Instead, create the perfect God Mode storm by:

- prioritising sleep and rest
- getting fresh air and exercise
- working intentionally
- planning your time wisely
- taking care of your mental health.

USE GOD MODE TO BUILD SYSTEMS FOR FUTURE-YOU

One of the best uses of God Mode is to make the most of that energy to support future-you:

- Create templates that take the brain function out of daily tasks.
- Set up automations to help your business run smoothly.
- Update those email flows.
- Tackle the jobs you have been putting off.

Reframing what you thought you knew

Yes, God Mode feels great when we're in it, but we need to understand that it's the first sign of burnout, or rather that wherever God Mode shows up, burnout is just around the corner.

Managing it when it arrives means that it will last longer and the crash will be less painful.

TL;DR

God Mode is a gift, but it's not meant to last, so use it wisely by focusing on high-impact work. Save the new ideas for later and build in recovery time and space.

You don't need to live in that state to run a successful business, you just need to work with it when it arrives so you don't pay the price of burnout when it leaves.

16

Don't tell me what to do

Demand avoidance

> **The goal with demand avoidance is to turn your 'demands' into options, so you never feel like you don't have the choice.**

Business is full of external demands, from clients, from our team, from the tax man ... the list goes on. Where previously you might have considered your resistance to these demands a character flaw, or passed it off as just being stubborn, it is actually a common experience with ADHD. Demand avoidance is a confusing and incredibly hard-to-explain phenomenon where we have something to do, we want to do that thing, but we simply cannot do it.

I have spoken to people who are at the point where they might have to get a job because their business isn't making money and the more they need to make money, the less they are able to do because the demand just feels so crushing.

When we think of demands we automatically think about practical things like tasks, but demand avoidance is so much more than that. It can be triggered by anything that feels like a demand on your time, energy, emotions or autonomy.

Social demands:

- Feeling pressure to reply to messages from friends.
- Avoiding phone calls or scheduled events, even with people you like.
- Cancelling plans even though you were looking forward to them.
- Getting overwhelmed by the expectation to 'show up' emotionally or socially.

Internal demands:

- 'I should be doing more.'
- 'I need to calm down.'
- 'I have to finish this book/podcast/course I started.'
- 'I really need to exercise.'

Emotional demands:

- Avoiding conversations that feel like they'll be intense or hard.
- Shutting down if it feels like someone expects you to explain your feelings or decisions.
- Feeling resistant to processing your emotions because it's just too much.

Authority-related demands:

- Letters from the tax man, your accountant, your kids' school or the dentist.

- Anything that feels like admin or too much responsibility can feel like a demand.
- Even being told to relax or 'just do it' by someone else can trigger resistance.

Sometimes, even doing something fun can feel like a demand if it's scheduled, someone else initiates it or you feel like you 'should' enjoy it.

In short, demand avoidance is about perceived pressure, not the task itself. Anything that pokes at your sense of autonomy, safety or capacity can become something to resist, even if it's something you genuinely want to do.

One of the most confusing aspects of demand avoidance is when you are about to do The Thing and someone reminds you about The Thing and the very fact that they've 'demanded' it of you means you can no longer do it.

Make it make sense!

It's worth mentioning at this point that demand avoidance is experienced by many people with ADHD, but PDA (pathological demand avoidance) is a more extreme version that is classed as a profile within the autism spectrum. PDA encompasses much more than avoiding everyday demands or tasks on your to-do list and is rooted in the need for autonomy. In fact, many people choose to use the term 'persistent desire for autonomy' instead of pathological demand avoidance as they feel it's a more accurate description of the experience.

I think it's worth distinguishing between demand avoidance and pathological demand avoidance because while they have very similar names, they are different experiences.

As someone who recognises PDA traits in myself, I can easily spot it in a client and will be extra mindful of how I communicate with them. I have a head start as I already avoid authoritarian language because it triggers me so much (for example, it drove me mad when my boss used to add 'for me' on to the end of every work-related request), but I will be extra cautious and extra collaborative in my approach.

So, what's going on? The ADHD connection

Demand avoidance isn't one single thing for ADHDers, it is a culmination of things, including perfectionism, anxiety, task initiation or switching, time scarcity, energy supply and routine disruption. Any one of these can build up to create what we have named demand avoidance. For me, with exercise, I realised it came down to time scarcity and transitioning (in this case getting changed, having a shower, getting dressed again).

The science behind demand avoidance is pretty complex, but it is increasingly understood as a protective response driven by nervous system dysregulation, executive function challenges and emotional sensitivity, especially in relation to autonomy and overwhelm.

As we know, the ADHD brain struggles with executive function – things like planning, starting, prioritising and following through. When a demand shows up (even something as small as 'reply to that email' or 'write that post'), the brain can instantly misjudge how hard it'll be or how long it'll take and begin to spiral, which triggers our threat response system.

The task – especially if it's imposed, urgent or emotionally loaded – feels overwhelming and so your nervous system kicks into survival mode: fight, flight, freeze or fawn (more on fawning in Chapter 19).

The difficulty is often not in the task but in the *feeling* behind it – if the demand comes with pressure, expectation or fear of judgement, the emotional stakes are heightened. And if rejection sensitivity and perfectionism are an issue for you, you might find yourself avoiding the task not because it's hard but because it feels like the outcome could reflect something about you.

That's why even things you want to do can be hard to start. Wanting isn't always enough when your brain perceives the demand as a threat to autonomy, safety or identity.

Our low dopamine levels also come in to play here as it means we are wired for autonomy, not obligation (i.e. the more externally imposed a task feels, the more likely we are to push back against it – or to shut down altogether).

So, if you've ever built up a task in your head, avoided it for days, then smashed it out in 20 minutes when you've finally decided the time is right, you can take some comfort in knowing that that wasn't a failure of willpower – it was your nervous system trying to protect you.

My Brain First journey: Working in a team

I'm going to tell you here that I recognise traits of PDA in myself, meaning I experience demand avoidance to an extreme extent. When I think back, I can link everything back to it, from being overweight, to struggling with authority in school, to defining myself as 'unemployable' because I found the hierarchy of the corporate world so challenging.

Whether it was a personal trainer doing literally what I was paying them to do and telling me to exercise, a teacher setting me work or a boss checking in, it felt uncomfortable beyond the usual 'this is annoying, leave me alone' response you would expect. I can even feel my nervous system feeling triggered (and not in a good way) by an advert that finishes with a call to action like 'go to this website now' or 'don't forget to book!'.

In business, this manifests for me in many ways, but one of the most challenging is that I struggle to work with people. And I know this is a common experience among many ADHD entrepreneurs.

Having problems working in a team isn't a huge problem in itself. Sure, it's a pain and can have business impacts, but if you know what's going on, then you can manage it. The issue arises when you don't know why you're being avoidant and you push on anyway.

I can think of countless times in the past – way before I knew I had ADHD, let alone understood PDA – where I would make a hire, believing this was the key to solving the current business bottleneck, only to find myself in a place of stalemate as

I shut down, struggling to take on board a new opinion and to communicate effectively in return. I learnt very early that my skills don't lie in people management, so it would rarely be the case that the new recruit would be depending on me for guidance or training (thank goodness!), but nevertheless my resistance to working collaboratively would present challenges and, internally, I would feel hugely conflicted as my nervous system struggled to cope.

Now I know more about this feeling and have the words to explain it, I have been able to manage it. I have found ways to work with people that don't trigger my PDA, but it hasn't been easy and I'm never far from a shame spiral around it.

Your Brain First business: Dealing with demand avoidance

Demand avoidance, especially in ADHD, is one of the trickiest, most misunderstood challenges. It's that *intense* internal resistance to doing something, even if you want to do it. It's not laziness or rebellion. It's your nervous system reacting to *the feeling of a demand*, not the task itself.

If you struggle with demand avoidance in your business, here are some strategies to try out. See what works for you, then add them to your Brain First Toolkit.

TURN DEMANDS INTO OPTIONS

Think about your to-do list and how the tasks you need to do are never the tasks you want to do. Under normal circumstances, that's ok. Even though they don't flood you with joy, you can still do them. It's when demand avoidance kicks in that they can feel almost impossible. When this happens, try the following:

- Options:
  - Rather than seeing your list as a to-do, start seeing it as a list of options. You will know which tasks need to be done and which are less of a priority, so there will be a natural order to this list. But the idea is that you can give yourself the autonomy to choose rather than feeling like a demand is placed on you.
- INCU:
  - This feeds into almost every aspect of ADHD, but especially demand avoidance. If you have a task that doesn't feed into one of these, then you don't stand a chance and are wasting your time even trying to get it done. Try sorting your tasks in order of urgency or interest (the two key players in INCU when it comes to tasks) and see how differently you feel about doing them.
- Rewards:
  - Avoid punishing yourself. As we've already discussed, that doesn't work for us and will just end up making you feel rubbish. Instead, set small rewards for completing tasks. Yes, I know this sounds patronising, but nothing puts a rocket up my ass like the promise of a trip to my favourite shop for lunch if I get a specific task done.

AGENCY AND AUTONOMY

If demand avoidance is a threat response, you need to understand what your brain is finding threatening about the task it's avoiding. Try asking yourself, 'What am I afraid of happening as a result of completing this task?' You might be surprised that the answer is what you think you want, i.e. 'I will win the contract' or 'I will be asked to speak at the event', or that concerns like perfectionism, unclear expectations, fear of being seen or task switching come up.

WORDS MATTER

Using words like 'I have to ...' or 'I should ...' can trigger avoidance, so remove them if you can. Language affects your nervous system, so make it gentler and more autonomous where possible. For example:

- 'I *get* to write this post.'
- 'I'm *choosing* to send this email so future-me is less stressed.'
- 'I *want* to try working on this for five minutes.'
- 'I'm *grateful* I get to move my body.'

USE MICRO-COMMITMENTS

Treat your brain like a toddler and help it by breaking down the task into the very first step. Just commit to starting rather than finishing the whole task. Once you're in motion, the task often loses its power over you. It might feel silly, but honestly it works:

- 'I'll just open the doc.'
- 'I'll just reply to one message.'
- 'I'll just set a five-minute timer.'

ADD NOVELTY INTO THE MIX

Novelty and play reduce threat, so gamify the demand and make it a challenge for your brain to complete:

- 'Can I do this task before the timer goes off?'
- 'What's the scrappiest version I can complete?'
- 'Can I "trick" myself into doing it by pretending it's for someone else?'

JUST (DON'T) DO IT!

This one is counterintuitive, but powerful. When your brain feels like it *has* to do something, it pushes back. So simply try tricking your brain by saying: 'I don't have to do this. I can choose to delay, delegate or delete it.' Often, that permission defuses the resistance enough to *start anyway*.

PLAN FOR IT

Finally, if you know you experience demand avoidance, give yourself a fighting chance by building your business with it in mind. Make sure you have:

- flexible deadlines
- overflow time
- gentle accountability
- systems and strategies that work for you (i.e. having an 'options list' instead of a 'task list', or filtering your tasks in order of urgency).

Reframing what you thought you knew

Demand avoidance is a natural and common experience among those with ADHD and fighting it will only make it worse.

It's almost always rooted in our need for autonomy and that isn't something to be ashamed of – being aware and working with it is the key to navigating it.

TL;DR

Demand avoidance isn't defiance, it's your brain protecting your autonomy, your energy or your nervous system.

The natural response when it crops up is to fight it, but that's the worst thing you can do. Having systems and strategies to go to and finding ways to lower the pressure and reclaim your agency is key.

17

But do you hate me?

The impact of rejection sensitive dysphoria

> **It's not just about being over sensitive or 'taking things personally'. It's a full-body, physical experience that feels like being unworthy, unlovable and unsafe, all at once.**

I love it when I speak to someone with ADHD who hasn't heard of rejection sensitive dysphoria because I know that it's very likely to be a huge lightbulb moment for them.

If you are one of those people, then tap in because this is a game changer!

RSD is an intense reaction to *perceived, actual or even anticipated* rejection, criticism or failure, triggering emotional (and physical) pain, shame or anger – often out of proportion to the situation.

It isn't a formal diagnosis (as in, it doesn't appear in the DSM, the internationally recognised diagnostic manual), but it's a well-known experience for many people with ADHD, and if you experience it then you will understand just how much it impacts your life. What you might not know, though, is how much it impacts your business.

If you are late diagnosed or identified then the truth is that we are just becoming used to the way our brain works. Most people I know (including myself) assumed that everyone felt the same about tricky moments and that we were all replaying a comment, change in facial expression or energy shift for weeks after the event, feeling crushed by minor feedback (even when constructive), and actively avoiding events or opportunities where we could be judged or 'found out'.

It's often the root cause of people-pleasing too, whereby we fall over ourselves to make others happy so they don't reject us, as well as its total opposite (rejecting them so they can't reject us first).

Have you ever done that thing where you are just going about your day and realise your mood has shifted and you feel angry or slightly anxious? Before I understood about RSD, I would get angry or anxious and believe that I was just 'moody' (another favourite childhood label), but once I understood how this chain of events worked, I knew something else was going on and I had to stop and rewind.

When I retrace my steps to understand what has happened to change my mood, nine times out of ten I can trace it back to an email, text message or even, and I'm not proud to admit this, a daydreamed scenario where someone has said something that has triggered my RSD.

In the case of the email or text message, it's usually that before I opened it, I decided it was going to say something awful – and *that* was what caused the distress (I'm pretty sure you do this, too).

RSD is particularly difficult to explain to anyone who doesn't experience it because it just sounds SO SILLY. But if you experience it, then it's not silly at all, it's very real, and for many can be the hardest part of ADHD to manage.

So, what's going on? The ADHD connection

Many people with a neurodivergent brain would class themselves as emotionally hypersensitive.

In the 90s, psychologists Elaine and Arthur Aron developed the term 'Highly Sensitive Person' (HSP) to describe someone who has increased emotional sensitivity, stronger reactivity to both internal and external stimuli such as pain, hunger, light and noise, and a rich, complex and noisy inner life.

This later became part of an umbrella of profile categories under SPS (sensory-processing sensitivity). This isn't a diagnosis and isn't classed as a neurodivergence, but in recent years – as the research around ADHD and autism has expanded (especially research around these profiles in women) – more and more people are understanding the crossover and the impact of emotional sensitivity issues in their day-to-day lives.

Although this is not at all scientific, I would say that for over 95 per cent of the female clients I have worked with, the business challenges that they wanted help with all boiled down to something relating to RSD.

Not hitting their business goals would very often shake out as a fear of rejection:

- Not promoting themselves online for fear of judgement.
- Not chasing down or following up opportunities for fear of a NO.
- Setting unrealistic targets as a way of self-sabotaging and rejecting themselves before anyone else can.
- Keeping themselves small so no one can criticise or judge.
- Working alone rather than coping with possible rejection from other people.

RSD is so sneaky, it will gaslight you, it will make you paranoid and it will lead you to act in ways that are irrational. None of which is helpful in business.

RSD feels intense for a reason – it's deeply tied to how your brain processes threat, emotion and self-worth. If you experience it then you're definitely not alone as approximately one-third of adults with ADHD say RSD is the most impairing part of their condition.[31]

For someone with RSD, the experience of rejection isn't just emotional, it's happening on a biological level. The brain reads rejection – even subtle or imagined – as a threat to belonging. And because belonging is wired into us as a core survival need, the response is instant and intense.

At the centre of this reaction is the amygdala (the brain's alarm system), which lights up fast when it senses danger. It's a little dramatic and tends to overreact, sending out a flood of cortisol and adrenaline (the stress hormones) to help the situation. This then triggers a full-body threat response, sending your nervous system into fight, flight or freeze.

Once that flood hits, the brain works hard to restore calm, but for people with ADHD that's where things get even trickier. The prefrontal cortex, responsible for regulating emotions and applying logic, is underdeveloped so doesn't always kick in quickly enough. So there is no time to process 'this isn't personal' – the brain spirals, feelings take over and before you know it you're in meltdown.

Dopamine also plays a part in this chemical process as it's tied to emotional resilience, so when we experience or imagine the rejection, it is crushing and takes longer to recover from. Praise, meanwhile, can feel euphoric, which is why people with RSD often chase the validation of praise and hide away from the threat of criticism or rejection.

And just to really make it fun, the brain is always looking for similar experiences to match up, so when a current experience feels like rejection, it will go into the memory network and find every other experience that has felt vaguely similar – a cross word, an 'off' look, a change in tone or energy – and use it as evidence for that's what you're experiencing.

RSD can keep us hypervigilant as we scan for rejection. When we have experienced it our whole lives – without having the words to understand or explain it – it becomes embedded in the stories we tell ourselves about not being good enough or not being popular.

Neuroscience has shown that social rejection activates the same brain regions as physical pain, so it makes sense that repeated experiences of being misunderstood or dismissed, which are especially common in ADHD, can lead to a deep sense of shame, self-doubt and emotional withdrawal.

My Brain First journey: More bloody labels

I first heard the term 'rejection sensitive dysphoria' around 2012 when I was running my first business and it absolutely floored me.

I was in a deep depression following my breakdown and was spending a large percentage of my time searching for the answer to 'what is wrong with me?'. I came across several possibilities. Borderline personality disorder largely fit my human experience, but not entirely, while depression and anxiety were already on my medical bingo card and had been on and off since I was 11. But I knew there was more to it.

ADHD wasn't spoken about outside of 'naughty boys and video games' back then, so it wasn't even a twinkle in my eye, but I came across an article on RSD and I had at least part of my answer. It explained so much.

I binged everything I could find on it – which wasn't a huge amount in all honesty – and took it to a therapist I'd recently started seeing. I was so excited to tell her my discovery. Maybe she hadn't heard of it either and she would be as fascinated as I was? Perhaps she would know all about it and really be able to help me make sense of myself.

I told her as soon as we sat down. 'I found some information about rejection sensitive dysphoria and I think that's what I have! It really feels like what I experience: the extreme sensitivity to people and their emotions, the difficulty I have had in interpersonal relationships and the way I people-please or shut down to avoid rejection.'

I looked at her, like the teacher's pet that just did all their homework. She rolled her eyes and said, 'There's a label for everything nowadays.'

Great ... now I had to find a new therapist, too.

That experience genuinely put me back so far. I forgot all about the term until I was looking into getting my diagnosis some eight years later. Seeing that it was one of the most common traits experienced by people with ADHD helped to convince me that I was ADHD too.

Your Brain First business: Handling RSD

If you experience RSD in your business, here are some practical strategies that you should try. Give them a go and add the ones that work to your Brain First Toolkit.

CURIOSITY OVER FEAR

The first thing to do is to stop and get curious about what is going on. A simple pause helps your brain shift from full-blown panic into curiosity and also gives you a second to question whether the reaction matches the reality. Try asking:

- 'What just happened to make me feel rejected?'
- 'Is it really a rejection or am I experiencing RSD?'

QUICK REALITY CHECK

I find it helpful to have a prompt or script in my Toolkit. Try a three-step script like this:

1. What actually happened?
2. What story am I telling myself about it?
3. What do I know to be true?

Example:

1. They didn't reply to my message.
2. I'm telling myself they're mad at me.
3. I know that I haven't done anything to upset them, so perhaps they are just busy.

BUILD A 'THIS IS WHO I AM' BANK

When you're spiralling, logic won't always make sense. Instead of relying on your brain for support, create a go-to kit that feels emotionally safe and brings you back to yourself:

- screenshots of kind feedback or testimonials
- a voice note from a friend hyping you up
- photos from fun trips with special people
- written reminders like 'this feeling is temporary'.

RESPOND, DON'T REACT

If you're feeling triggered by an email, don't reply when your chest is tight, your heart is racing and your brain's memory network is telling you to respond in the same way you did last time. Step away first and take a pause. This isn't avoidance, it's regulating before you re-engage. Try:

- going for a walk
- a cold water splash
- box breathing (inhale for a count of four, hold for four, exhale for four, hold for four)
- going to your 'this is who I am' bank (see above).

KNOW YOUR DEMONS

Understand your triggers and the things that are most likely to send you into a spiral. Once you know them, create a response plan – who you'll talk to, what you'll do, how you'll ground. This isn't about avoiding triggers, it's about being prepared for when they inevitably happen. Example triggers could include:

- someone unfollowing you on social media
- a vague message like 'can we talk?'
- feedback on something you poured your heart into.

ASK FOR CLARITY

People with RSD tend to over-communicate to seek reassurance or under-communicate out of fear. When we're experiencing an RSD attack, it might feel hard to press for clarity, but you owe it to yourself and to the other person to try. Practise simply asking: 'Can I clarify what you meant by that?' Get clarity and kill the spiral before it starts.

PROTECT YOUR NERVOUS SYSTEM

RSD can be so damaging in business, it will stop you from reaching your goals and hold you back in every area if you let it. If you regularly find yourself:

- checking email obsessively after sending a pitch
- over-apologising for things that weren't your fault
- not launching a product or service because you're afraid people will hate it
- creating content and never posting it because 'who cares?'

try building in some buffer systems:

- Pre-schedule content so you don't obsess over it.
- Create a character. I used to have an 'assistant' way before I could afford an assistant. She was called 'Jess' and when I needed to respond to my customer service emails, I would imagine I was Jess when replying – the psychological distance was life changing!

Reframing what you thought you knew

RSD isn't about being 'too sensitive'. It's a legitimate pain response from an ADHD nervous system that's wired for emotional intensity. With awareness, tools and boundaries, you can learn to respond instead of react.

While it would be a stretch to say RSD is a positive in business, if it's understood and contained rather than just allowed to spiral, it does mean we lead with empathy and sensitivity to others.

TL;DR

Being sensitive isn't a moral issue, you aren't good or bad for feeling things more than others. However, you should make sure you understand your triggers and build supportive strategies into your life to help, so that you are not debilitated by your RSD.

18

I like you, do you like me?

How our people-pleasing tendencies are keeping us broken

> **"Radical acceptance, boundary setting and self-compassion are key to putting yourself first in your business and helping you to realise that putting yourself first is actually the least selfish thing you can do.**

A lifetime of being made to feel like too much, not enough and everything in between has helped many of us build a nervous system that equates safety with keeping other people happy, and our behaviour reflects that.

If you are a people-pleaser then you will be familiar with the constant hypervigilance: scanning every room you're in for how people interact with you, checking to see if their mood, tone or energy are changing, and trying to address any concerns straight away – which all means falling into people-pleasing patterns and repertoires you have come to rely on.

In life, this can be problematic; in business, disastrous. It leads to terrible decisions, miscommunication through conflict avoidance and is the main culprit behind your imposter syndrome.

Do you remember the statistic from Part I that told us that by the age of ten, kids with ADHD receive 20,000 more negative messages than their neurotypical peers? That is seriously damaging to such a young and impressionable mind. If you don't yet know that you have ADHD and so don't have a reason for why you are lazy/slow/distracted/flaky/untrustworthy/away with the fairies/a liar (delete as appropriate), then it's very easy to interpret those words as the truth, internalise the judgement they are delivered with and turn it into shame.

This is the first building block of our people-pleasing trauma response.

Here's a hard pill to swallow (brace yourself for this one): people-pleasing is actually a form of control. Think about the way you feel when you begin to people-please, that sensation in the pit of your stomach, rising heart rate, racing mind, elevated temperature – that, my friend, is anxiety.

If we have come to believe that someone being unhappy with us makes us unsafe, then the moment our 'spidey senses' detect (or assume) that this is happening, we become anxious and look for ways we can make things safe again – namely, by controlling the environment/people around us. So, we offer them food or a drink, tell a joke, pay them a compliment – anything to change the way we are feeling and return to safety. And on the face of it, this is great – these are all good ways to build relationships in life and in business. But these small, unharmful dopamine hits left unchecked can turn into the toxic people-pleasing habits that so many of us have come to rely on.

In business, people-pleasing can look like:

- saying yes to too much
- over-delivering out of guilt
- struggling to set or enforce boundaries
- avoiding difficult conversations
- taking responsibility for how other people feel.

This is all a slippery slope to burnout, resentment and that 'stuck' feeling where you start to lose sight of your vision because you're operating from fear, not strategy.

Let's take a look for a moment at the late-diagnosed/late-identified experience of thinking you've been pleasing people your whole life, then realising you have actually pleased no one, least of all yourself. When you have been operating under the assumption that you think pretty much the same way as everyone else and then *record scratch* realise that's not true, that's a pretty big adjustment.

So, what's going on? The ADHD connection

The science behind people-pleasing is rooted in a mix of nervous system survival responses, emotional regulation challenges and sometimes low self-worth or rejection sensitivity. This is especially common in ADHD, autism or trauma backgrounds, and particularly in women.

When it comes to nervous system responses, most people know about fight, flight or freeze. But there's a lesser-known fourth response: fawn.

Fawning is 'appeasing others to avoid conflict, rejection or emotional discomfort'.[32] It's a survival strategy, often learnt early in life, especially in unpredictable or emotionally unsafe environments, so if your nervous system detects a social threat (even just a critical tone or disapproval), it might try to 'keep the peace' by defaulting to fawning, i.e. people-pleasing.

We know by now that our brains are incredible, complicated things that are running the show, so this is what is going on in there when we start to people-please:

- Amygdala: this is overactive in people who are sensitive to perceived rejection or social threat and this is the area that triggers the fawn response.
- Prefrontal cortex: this is the bit responsible for boundaries and reasoning. If it's not regulating the amygdala well (which is common with ADHD), you might know you're people-pleasing by over-committing but feel powerless to stop it.
- Insula: this area is tied to shame and social pain. As people-pleasers, we often experience discomfort when we feel that we aren't meeting others' expectations.

You can add to this the uber dopamine boost we get from external validation and, on the flip side, the pain we feel when we receive criticism – so, saying yes gives us an extra dopamine hit (approval, praise, inclusion) and saying no means risk of disapproval (which equals stress, which equals a dopamine crash). Knowing this, it's no wonder that over time, your brain learns to seek safety in compliance and through over-extending ... even if it hurts you.

As already mentioned, people-pleasing is often an adaptive technique learnt in childhood, perhaps as a consequence of inconsistent or critical caregivers, conditional love or attention, or early trauma and bullying. In all those cases, people-pleasing becomes a way to stay safe and connected because being liked means being protected.

My Brain First journey: Recovering people-pleaser

I would call myself a chronic people-pleaser and yet, when I look around at the people I have actually pleased, there are very few.

Before I had my ADHD diagnosis, I assumed everyone operated the way I operated, so if something upset me, I believed that my feelings were valid and that everyone else would feel the same in that situation. What I didn't realise was that I was often experiencing RSD and many times was blowing up a simple miscommunication into something that was never meant at all.

When this happened I would just cut the other person off. For ever.

This has led to a lifetime of difficult interpersonal relationships and feelings that are complicated and hard to manage. I know I'm not alone in dealing with this. So many people I speak to or work with would also class themselves as people-pleasers and also deal with difficult relationship patterns, and it makes perfect sense why.

We know that ADHD is largely genetic and so was kindly gifted to us by one or perhaps both of our parents. Because of the time we are living in, and the fact that we are still researching neurodivergent conditions, particularly in adults and especially in women, our parents were unlikely to have been diagnosed or even aware that their brain was different from other people's and that their 'personality quirks' were in fact ADHD or autism.

Now, this isn't an easy conversation to have because many people assume that there is an element of blame inferred when we start talking about our childhood, but I think that our awareness of undiagnosed neurodivergent conditions, and the compassion we can hold around that, removes any blame entirely.

I can only speak for myself here (and I am aware perhaps that you will be reading this thinking, 'no, my parents were arseholes, and should have protected me better. They are entirely to blame', and if that is true, then I'm sorry) but in my case, and the case of many of the people I work with, we grew up in loving, well-intentioned homes. We were cared for, provided for and, on the whole, kept safe. But we cannot deny the fact that if our parents had undiagnosed neurodevelopmental conditions, then their emotional dysregulation, executive function and own trauma responses or coping mechanisms would have impacted us greatly.

It would have impacted our attachment style from birth, it would have impacted our sense of safety, our self-esteem and our world view.

Now, let's not forget that I am talking about growing up in the 80s – it was a different time and therapy speak wasn't a thing. But that's another reason why there is no blame. It's just that many parents were dealing with undiagnosed ADHD/autism and were confused and overwhelmed, while also raising a child or children with undiagnosed ADHD/autism who was/were confused and overwhelmed and relying on them for a sense of safety.

I'm not a therapist, or a scientist, but I can see an undeniable link between neurodivergent children raised by (largely undiagnosed/unaware) neurodivergent parents who were overwhelmed and perhaps less able to provide the emotional safety needed to raise a child with a nervous system that feels 'safe' and doesn't spend the rest of their life seeking that safety through external validation, i.e. people-pleasing.

I'm so grateful that we have the understanding and information to start to unpick this stuff and to understand how we got to the place we now find ourselves.

So, one thing you are going to have to do if you are serious about creating a better business is fight against your people-pleasing with every ounce of teenage angst you can still muster.

Your Brain First business: Moving on from people-pleasing

If people-pleasing is one of your more damaging coping strategies, then take a look at the suggestions below and test them out to spot it, stop it and shift it – without blowing up your business or relationships.

As ever, add the ones that work to your Brain First Toolkit to come back to when you need them.

KNOW YOUR PATTERNS

Awareness is always step one – you can't set a boundary if you don't know where it's being crossed, so start by identifying how it shows up for you and where this is a problem in your business. Some common, but sneaky, ways we muddy our own boundaries are:

- saying yes on impulse, then instantly regretting it
- over-delivering to avoid criticism
- discounting or undercharging to 'be nice'
- feeling resentment but pushing through anyway
- avoiding feedback or conflict at all costs.

UNDERSTAND IT

There is always an underlying emotion that's driving your people-pleasing, so next time you feel that anxiety rising and the temptation to fawn, ask yourself: 'What am I afraid will happen if I say no?' Often the fear is rejection, judgement or being seen as 'difficult'. Once you spot the story, you can start understanding what is really going on. Remember: using 'no' makes your 'yesses' more meaningful.

CREATE STOCK PHRASES

If you know that you are prone to a panic 'yes' on the spot, buy yourself time by creating stock phrases to fall back on. This disrupts the autopilot 'yes' and gives you a window to decide *on your terms*. Try some of these:

- 'Let me check my calendar and get back to you.'
- 'Can I think about that and let you know?'
- 'I just need to check what I have on so I know I can fully commit.'

STOP

Before you let your impulse kick in with an instant 'yes', ask:

- Do I want to do this?
- Do I have capacity to do this?
- Would I say yes if I weren't afraid of letting them down?
- If this was tomorrow, would I want to do it?

If it's a 'no' but you're struggling to say it, write it down and sit with it before responding or buy yourself some time with one of your stock phrases.

AUTOMATE BUSINESS BOUNDARIES

Don't leave it to your brain to kick in and set boundaries, review your client or stakeholder touchpoints and give them the information they need to know. This not only sets the stage for success, it also gives you both something to refer to if any conflict arises.

- Client onboarding doc: add clear response times, hours you are available.
- Project scope docs: outline project schedule and timelines to avoid over-delivery or confusion.
- Pricing sheets: set as standard so you're not negotiating on the fly.

KNOW WHAT'S YOURS

People-pleasing often stems from not knowing how to sit with other people's discomfort after a lifetime of feeling that these situations have always been your fault. Remember: you're responsible for how you act, not how they react. Try a simple reframe like: 'Someone else feeling disappointed doesn't mean I did something wrong.'

VALUE YOURSELF UNCONDITIONALLY

I'm going to hold your hand because this is the biggie: if you tie your worth to how liked you are, you'll always over-give to earn approval. Try shifting your perspective with some simple language changes. For example, in a new client meeting, move your internal monologue from 'I hope they like me' to 'I hope this is the right fit for both of us'.

PRACTISE BOUNDARY SETTING

I know it sounds silly, but if you think you're going to go from chronic people-pleasing to holding firm boundaries overnight then you're setting yourself up to fail. Practise setting easy boundaries with yourself or friends first. Remember that saying 'no' will feel hard to start with but, like any habit, will get easier over time.

PRACTISE NON-TOXIC PEOPLE-PLEASING

This is my favourite way to channel my people-pleasing – it feels good for everyone and leaves you with a little dopamine boost without doing yourself any harm. Try these:

- helping someone elderly up stairs or across the road
- engaging in really active listening with a friend
- doing a 'random act of kindness' for a client or team member.

The key here is that they are things you have consciously decided to do, not been triggered into by your nervous system.

Reframing what you thought you knew

Radical acceptance, boundary setting and self-compassion are key to putting yourself first in your business and helping you to realise that putting yourself first is actually the least selfish thing you can do.

TL;DR

People-pleasing is a symptom of a nervous system that feels unsafe.

In life it can be a pain, but in business, disastrous, so it's important to keep those small people-pleasing dopamine hits in check so they don't escalate to toxic people-pleasing that prioritises everyone above you.

19

The burnout trap

Coping with burnout

> **What if ADHD wasn't leading you to burnout but it was simply the fact that you are putting yourself in the wrong environment and trying to keep up with a set of rules that were never designed for you?**

Once again for the people at the back: business standards are neurotypical standards and by trying to reach them with a neurodivergent brain, we expose ourselves to damaging amounts of overwhelm, dysregulation and exhaustion.

Until we accept that not everybody's working day, productivity and capacity for workload looks the same, we will continue to be disadvantaged by our susceptibility to burnout.

Burnout has become a catch-all term for reaching breaking point in our business, but we often don't recognise it until we hit capital 'B' Burnout, completely disregarding the baby 'b' burnout dominoes that we knocked over on our way.

That cute afternoon slump that we think we can fix with a KitKat and a can of Diet Coke? Yep, that's burnout.

That Friday feeling when you can't string a sentence together and just want to reach for the wine? That's burnout, too.

And the truth is that most of us are living in Functional Burnout and are, at any given moment, just a few distractions, triggers or misaligned tasks away from the crash.

The dilemma with ADHD and burnout is that we often need danger dopamine to get anything done, so we will take on a bit too much, commit to an unrealistic deadline or agree to something that is out of our comfort zone, just to get our brain firing. But do we really know our brain well enough to know what *is just enough* and what will actually tip us over the edge?

Even that isn't a clear-cut question because what feels like a small stretch one day might feel like just too much another. That can be down to so many factors: energy levels, hormones, workload, mental health ... the list goes on.

While I'm delighted that the general LinkedIn narrative has moved past us wearing burnout like some kind of entrepreneurial badge of honour, I do think that we accept it as a necessary evil – just part of the road to our chosen business destination and something we have to find a way to handle rather than work to prevent.

But that is exactly what we should be working towards: a business that *prevents* burnout as much as possible, one where we build our own protocols to manage our baby 'b' burnouts, recognising them as the signposts and immediately knowing we have to stop them in their tracks.

So, what's going on? The ADHD connection

ADHD burnout comprises these three key areas:

- Physical exhaustion: constant full body fatigue.
- Cognitive weariness: brain fog and reduced mental clarity caused by over-extending.
- Emotional depletion: irritability, overwhelm, guilt, shame caused by daily triggers.

We know only too well our struggles with planning, prioritising and sustaining focus when it comes to ADHD, but a study actually found that our deficits in executive function are the bridge in the relationship between ADHD and burnout. Essentially, the brain's constant effort to stay organised and on-task depletes our mental resources, which then leads to exhaustion and burnout.[33]

Even routine tasks demand far more mental energy for us than they do for a neurotypical brain. We're not just completing a task, we're also resisting distractions and managing impulses. Dealing with that constant internal conflict leads to mental fatigue, which is another domino down on the path to burnout. And while hyperfocus can feel like our secret weapon, those intense focus sessions can lead to us neglecting our basic needs: sleep, food, hydration and rest breaks. So, when the hyperfocus ends, you crash physically and emotionally with a burnout hangover and wonder if it was all worth it.

A 2017 study found that burnout hits people with ADHD at three times the rate of the general population: ~54 per cent vs 18 per cent.[34] This isn't a surprise, but it should be. We have to accept that burnout isn't just part of the journey and start seeing it as a problem we have to fix.

The extra kicker with burnout is that once it happens, it's extra hard for us to find a route through. Have you heard of object permanence? It's a childhood developmental milestone that marks the understanding that objects still exist even when you can't see them (it's why we play 'peekaboo' with toddlers). Well, with ADHD we experience this in reverse. 'If it's not here right now, it doesn't exist.' It's why we don't take the supplements that are in the drawer, or we can have a smoothie every day for a month but then as soon as we put the blender in the cupboard we forget smoothies ever existed.

This phenomenon can apply to our emotions as well. So, when we are ill, or in a period of burnout, or bad mental health, we feel as though that is how we will always feel. It's like we forget being well is an option. This can make the experience so much worse as it's hard to see the light at the end of the tunnel. It really helps to know that this will happen because it feels so real when you're in the moment. Being aware, applying a little kindness and logic and reminding yourself this is temporary and you will get better can really make a difference.

My Brain First journey: Fear of burning out

Burnout was my baseline for so long, I thought it was just the price you paid for 'success'. I didn't realise that my burnout was different from the burnout other people talked about, and just how much long-term damage I was doing to my nervous system by ignoring it and limping on through it.

It's this pattern that led me to my big, huge, capital B burnout where I ended up in my childhood bed for ten weeks – and while I do consider that to be a breakdown, the cause of it was, with absolutely no doubt, burnout itself. I had been working too hard, for too long, ignoring my own needs and punishing myself for not being neurotypical by trying to squeeze my square peg into every round hole in my business. Dealing with conflict, and ultimately trying to keep a dying business alive, I had been feeding the company's life support with my own energy – energy that I just didn't have every day.

Bearing in mind that was a good eight years before my diagnosis, it took me until I understood more about ADHD and my brain to recognise just how much that episode has impacted the way I run my businesses now. And once I saw it, I saw it in so many people I worked with, it was kind of impossible to ignore. Identifying it seemed to have such a positive impact on my clients, so hopefully it will with you, too.

When you're in a burnout spell, you often cope simply because you don't have a choice. It's pure hell, and everything suffers. If you're self-employed, you have to make a choice between pushing through and making the episode worse or taking time off to recuperate and making no money. If you have a team then you have to find the energy to effectively communicate what you are going through so you can step back and keep the wheels turning.

Coming out the other end, however, that is when you experience what I have coined FOBO: the Fear Of Burning Out.

I'm sure the more accurate term would be PTSD because what we are actually experiencing is a full body 'there is no f*cking way I am EVER going back there' response, and it impacts every bit of our work forever more.

I will speak to people who tell me about their burnout episode from 10–15 years ago and you can see the horror wash over them as they recall it, usually framing it in the context of why they aren't setting bigger goals, or making more money, or growing a team – because they are terrified to return to that time and feel those feelings again.

They are living in FOBO and usually don't realise how it's impacting their choices, even now.

If you have been through burnout, stop and think about all the obvious – and the subtle – ways it impacts your business and therefore your potential success today.

It's in the way you compare your success to strangers online, or shy away from the big ideas that excite you so much, sticking to the safety of your comfort zone rather than grabbing that opportunity, or accepting the invitation, or doing the damn thing.

It doesn't all have to be negative though. I try to use my FOBO to remind me to set goals and run my businesses in ways that are sustainable.

I avoid working with big teams, I track my energy and hormones to better manage my workload and avoid my personal tipping point, and I am hyperaware of calendar bottlenecks and over-committing my time because they are the key things that have tripped me up before. Just like any kind of PTSD, our past experiences become our triggers, so we either work with them or build a life that avoids them.

Your wider lifestyle commitments also come into this. Before I became a mum, I took more risks and I would ignore some of the warning signs in my business when I could see I was approaching burnout. But now I know that it doesn't matter how burnt out I am or how much I need my personal space, my three-foot-tall sleep thief will still think I am his personal climbing frame – and so he should.

I won't let him pay the price for my lack of boundaries, so I have to leave a little bit extra in the tank and not let myself dance the burnout line anywhere near as closely as I used to.

Your Brain First business: Beating burnout

Burnout with ADHD isn't just about being tired, it's often the result of masking, pushing through executive dysfunction, context switching, perfectionism and not building enough recovery into your workflow.

Here are some of my go-to strategies for reducing burnout. Try them and stick the ones that work in your Brain First Toolkit.

IDENTIFY IT

The first step in combating burnout is to identify it. ADHD burnout can cleverly disguise itself as:

- brain fog
- emotional shutdown
- zero motivation for stuff you usually love.

Ask yourself: 'Am I physically exhausted, emotionally numb or just mentally overstimulated?' Identifying the type of burnout you're experiencing helps you know what kind of action you need to take.

STOP. IMMEDIATELY.

This isn't the time to 'push through' and make it work. Cancel non-essential meetings, pause launches and push deadlines. No one will thank you for being a hero when you're collapsed in bed because you didn't listen to your body.

REDUCE COGNITIVE LOAD

Burnout can come from decision fatigue and executive function overload. Try reducing those micro decisions you face every day and give your brain a chance to recover. Try these:

- Eat the same lunch every day for a week.
- Wear a 'uniform', i.e. wear the same clothes every day.
- Keep a 'minimum viable day' with a list of 2–3 non-negotiables and nothing else.

ACTIVE RELAXATION

Sorry to break it to you but scrolling, background Netflix and TikTok binges don't actually recharge your nervous system – but that doesn't mean you have to be lying horizontal either.

ADHD brains need more intentional stillness than we think and 'active relaxation' is a great way to reset your nervous system and start to come back to yourself.

How about:

- going on 'naked' nature walks: no headphones or distractions
- lying down with no stimulation
- enjoying silence – get used to not having constant input
- gentle sensory moments (try a warm bath or soft-textured clothing).

REVIEW YOUR BURNOUT

When you've recovered from a period of burnout, run a debrief to understand the chain of events that led you there. This might sound silly, but you might be surprised by the findings:

- What tipped me into burnout?
- What warning signs did I ignore?
- What was I doing out of obligation, not alignment?
- What would I do differently next time?

BABY STEPS

We have a tendency to charge back into things once we feel the fog lifting. Don't. Treat it like you would a 'phased return' in a job and give your nervous system a chance to heal. Try:

- half days for a week
- limiting yourself to one main task per day

- no meetings unless absolutely necessary
- avoiding all the tasks that got you into burnout for two weeks.

SWITCH YOUR GOALS

Start building your plan around your energy and capacity rather than your goals. Try switching from outcome to output goals which feel lighter and give you space to listen to your brain. For example:

- Outcome: 'Finish the launch by Friday.'
- Output: 'Spend 90 mins working on the launch today.'

CREATE A SAFETY NET

Put systems in place that detect when your next crash is about to happen and trigger your toolkit to support you through it. You could try:

- building from a minimum viable day to a 'minimum viable week' which features just business-critical tasks
- delegation or automation of any task that feels too much
- regular energy check-ins: 'how do I feel? What needs adjusting?'

GET HELP

While therapy is great, that's maybe not what you need right now. You might just need someone to:

- take over your inbox for three days
- body double while you tackle some overdue tasks
- help you make a decision when you're frozen by talking it through with you.

Get really granular. Don't just say, 'I'm burnt out', say, 'I need someone to help me with [specific task].'

Reframing what you thought you knew

What if ADHD wasn't leading you to burnout but it was simply the fact that you are putting yourself in the wrong environment and trying to keep up with a set of rules that were never designed for you?

You know the saying, 'When a flower doesn't bloom, you fix the environment in which it grows, not the flower'? Well yeah, exactly that.

We need to see burnout for what it truly is: our brain's way of saying, 'Something isn't working for me here and I'm going to give you a few warning signs, but I really need you to listen to them.'

TL;DR

Burnout is a warning sign that you're doing something wrong.

Many people think that burnout is horizontal bed rest, but (little b) burnout happens monthly, weekly or even daily. Catching those moments can reduce the chances of (big B) Burnout happening.

Conclusion
I love me: Acceptance and compassion

> **The negative space around the vacuum our people-pleasing creates is formed by the lack of love we have for ourselves.**

If you have read the previous chapters, then it will be abundantly clear why we struggle with self-compassion. But just to really labour the point: you have been raised in a world that wasn't designed for you, with little understanding of your needs, surrounded by people who had unrealistic expectations of you. And you've got to be some kind of zen hero to truly love yourself after going through that.

In the words of RuPaul, 'If you can't love yourself, how in the hell are you gonna love somebody else?'[35] How can we truly be the best leader, partner or friend if we can't heal the parts of us that got broken along the way?

It's kind of heartbreaking to realise, isn't it? But I find so much comfort, joy and hope in the speed at which research into and understanding of neurodivergence is developing. Don't get me wrong, we have a long, long way to go, but the access to community, information and support we now have is immense – whether you have the budget for private help or not, there are social media pages, groups and spaces where you belong and where you will find advice and guidance.

I hope that having read this book you will have gained an understanding of yourself that you didn't have previously. That you have found the permission you have been searching for. That you feel seen, and empowered enough to go and make things happen.

I work with brilliant, intelligent, creative and capable people day in, day out, who have started and failed, started and succeeded, given up, kept going when they shouldn't have – and everything in between. I often think about what the world would look like if all that potential was supported enough to bring their incredible ideas, strategic vision, creative dot-joining and laser-focused insights to life.

And I mean truly supported: so, given the unconditional love and safety to build confidence and self-esteem by their parents; nurtured for their skills at school and not berated for their weaknesses; put in education systems that allow for flexible assessment rather than one-size-fits-all silent exam rooms with vague questions on a paper; provided with the early career advice to support their interests rather than tick government boxes.

My sister and her husband are teachers and it's good to hear how much has already changed for young people growing up in today's systems, but we are still a million miles away from accepting that people have different brains and that that is something to be celebrated, not questioned.

I was featured in a *Daily Mail* article in 2025,[36] calling me a 'sickfluencer', and insinuating that I was in some way promoting ADHD and teaching people how to claim government grants. The comment section racked up more than 1,000 predictably angry entries, with everything from 'why does everyone need a label these days??' to those accusing me of the downfall of humanity.

While it's easy to see purposely divisive and clickbait articles like this and feel as though we are fighting a losing battle, doubted and challenged at every opportunity for finally understanding why our brain behaves the way it does, there is so much power in owning what is ours, taking responsibility for understanding it and consciously deciding how we will use it.

I firmly believe that neuroinclusivity in the workplace is no longer a diversity policy or a tick box, but a success strategy. In the same way that our farmers are working to encourage biodiversity, our leaders should be working to encourage neurodiversity, building teams that are fully diverse across race, gender, age and neurotype. This isn't a charity request, this is a challenge to see how bland and boring their teams are without our contribution.

But you don't get ADHD magic without supporting our weaknesses – just because we can do a day's work in two hours doesn't mean we can do that four times in a working day.

In a volatile, AI-driven world, divergent thinking will become a high-value, artisan skill – rare, human and in demand. Now isn't the time for us to sit back and lick our wounds but to recognise our strengths, grab them by the balls and shine a light on them, because we have the power to do that. As entrepreneurs, founders and leaders we don't have to wait for a big boss to ok an initiative to encourage neurodivergent employees – we can decide, today, to champion ourselves and each other.

That starts by creating a business that works for your brain – and that, as you now know, is your Brain First business.

Listen, I understand how easy it is to read this stuff and think 'yes, amazing!' ... and then go back to old patterns, but I really want you to take this on board and make some changes. It's honestly the only way that you are going to get out of that burnout cycle and get back some energy to actually live your life.

Start small, start today.

Maybe start here?

It's hard to make significant, impactful changes if we are working from a place of fear. In this final chapter, I want to teach you how radical self-acceptance and compassion are the necessary foundations for change.

Radical self-acceptance and self-love aren't just Instagram affirmations. They're acts of rebellion when you've spent your life feeling *too much*, *not enough* or *never quite right*. Especially for us, where masking, shame, inconsistency and internalised failure narratives run deep.

If I know anything about you, I know that acceptance and compassion aren't currently your strongest foundations, so here are some parting words to help you get there – please take them on board and please add them to your Brain First Toolkit.

You really deserve this.

START WITH SELF-AWARENESS

Self-love isn't about 'fixing yourself enough to feel worthy'. Radical self-acceptance starts when you stop trying to become *better* and start trying to become *more honest*. Try asking: 'What if nothing about me needs to be fixed but rather, understood?'

RATE YOUR TRAITS

Look at the traits you have been taught to hate or feel ashamed of. Write them out: the messiness, the emotional intensity, the impulsivity, the dreaming, the too much-ness. Then ask: 'When has this trait helped me?'; 'Where in my business is this actually a strength in disguise?' Did that high-energy, throw-yourself-instinct impress an investor and win you that pitch? Did your enthusiasm for a new idea infect your team and bring out the best in others, too?

NAME YOUR INNER CRITIC

This is a great tactic and one I use regularly: listen to that voice that doubts you, questions your actions, interrupts you mid-flow to challenge you, then identify it and give it a name.

This makes it easy to pick up quickly and easier to tell it to shut up. Your inner critic is usually the voice of an unkind family member, nasty teacher or toxic boss, so see if you can work out who yours is and take that power away from it.

Once you've identified it and named it, then you can start changing the way it speaks to you and so make your internal dialogue a safe place – not another battleground.

FEEL YOUR FEELINGS

We will often suppress feelings until we explode, but self-love means holding space for all of you – even the messy, loud, scared, numb parts. In fact, especially those parts.

Allow yourself to move through your emotions: cry, rage, nap, journal, walk, talk. But don't shut yourself down or bypass your emotions with unhelpful strategies. Try to feel them in your whole body – sense where they are and be extra gentle with yourself as you let them pass through you.

CATCH THE SHAME

Shame hates to see self-compassion coming, so identify those sneaky shame signals early so you can head them off and make more way for the good stuff!

Shame can be hiding in:

- 'I should be further ahead.'
- 'I mess everything up.'
- 'Everyone else has it figured out but me.'

When it does hit, respond with curiosity, not judgement: 'What is the belief I have about myself right now?'; 'Where did I learn that and is it still true?'

WHAT ARE YOU TRYING TO PROVE?

Do you really need to be the best? Always the most helpful? Never a burden to others? Perfectly 'healed'? That's not love, that's performance. Radical acceptance means choosing yourself, even if it disappoints others in the process – and that's not easy to digest. When you feel the need to be better, or more, ask yourself: 'If I let go of this belief, what would change?'

BUILD A BRAIN FIRST LIFE

Self-love isn't set and forget, it's a daily choice and commitment to yourself. There is no question of whether you deserve it or if it's self-indulgent – it's a non-negotiable, and your new normal. It looks like:

- saying 'no' when your body says 'no' – and meaning it
- designing your life around your actual needs, not the version of you you're 'supposed' to be.

Reframing what you thought you knew

Radical self-acceptance means giving yourself the love, permission and protection you've always given everyone else. You don't have to earn it, you just have to decide you're done performing and are ready to come home to yourself.

It will feel uncomfortable and you will have days when you just want to crawl into a ball of familiar self-loathing, but I promise you that radical self-awareness and compassion are the keys to implementing the important learnings in this book and making them stick.

And if I know anything about you after spending all these chapters of this book with you, it's that you deserve it.

TL;DR

Radical self-acceptance and compassion are the keys to building a Brain First business and a life that you have the energy to enjoy.

Don't stay sitting on the sidelines watching everyone else play the game, this is your invitation to join us.

And so to one final exercise.

Your Brain First business: How to overcome blocks and avoid the return to bad habits

This template will help you work through any blocks that come up as you try to work steadily and consistently towards your goals. It will give you something to refer to as and when you recognise old habits sneaking back in.

We start with a worked example to show you how you can identify problems, understand them, think how to better align them with your own needs and what you can do to put positive change into action.

Print off a sheet or go to the toolkit and complete one for every challenge you come up against in your business.

EXAMPLE: I HATE 'LAUNCHING' A NEW PRODUCT

What is happening:

- I have a launch plan that makes sense on paper but I hate putting myself out there to actually do it.

Awareness (what you now see is going on):

- Launching is triggering my RSD and also makes me feel incredibly vulnerable and exposed, which triggers my demand avoidance. This makes me feel unsafe, so I hate doing it.

Alignment (how you can make this work for your brain):

- Instead of launching products to my whole audience, I am going to focus on building outreach to my email list so I can just sell to people who I know are already interested.

Action (what steps you need to take):

- Create a valuable free offer to attract high-quality email subscribers so I have more people to 'launch' to.
- Focus my content on attracting new people rather than just building connections with my existing audience.

Notes:
I don't have to do it the way THEY do it. It is fine for me to find what works for me.

MY CHALLENGE

What is happening:

____

____

Awareness (what you now see is going on):

____

____

Alignment (how you can make this work for your brain):

____

____

Action (what steps you need to take):

____

____

Notes:

Notes

1 Daniel A. Lerner et al., 'Entrepreneurship and attention deficit/hyperactivity disorder: A large-scale study involving the clinical condition of ADHD', *Small Business Economics* 53, 381–392 (2019), https://doi.org/10.1007/s11187-018-0061-1

2 Kyle Pearce, '10 facts about ADHD, neurodiversity and entrepreneurship', ADHD Flow State, accessed/modified 22 August 2024, https://www.adhdflowstate.com/facts-about-adhd-neurodiversity-and-entrepreneurship/

3 Gino Wickam and Mack C. Winters, *Rocket Fuel: The one essential combination that will get you more of what you want from your business* (Benbella Books, 2015)

4 '10 famous people who had ADHD and made it their superpower', Body + Mind, accessed/modified 3 September 2025, https://bodymind.com/famous-people-who-had-adhd/

5 Michael S. Jellinek, 'Don't let ADHD crush children's self-esteem', MDedge, accessed/modified 1 May 2010, https://cdn.mdedge.com/files/s3fs-public/issues/articles/70231_main_7.pdf

6 Saul MacLeod, 'Maslov's Hierarchy of Needs', *Simply Psychology*, 3 August 2025

7 Anthony Yeung et al., 'TikTok and attention-deficit/hyperactivity disorder: A cross-sectional study of social media content quality', *The Canadian Journal of Psychiatry*, 67(12), 899–906 (23 February), https://pubmed.ncbi.nlm.nih.gov/35196157/

8 Mai Uchida et al., 'The heritability of ADHD in children of ADHD parents: A post-hoc analysis of longitudinal data',

Journal of Attention Disorders, 27(3), 250–257, https://doi.org/10.1177/10870547221136251 (original work published 2023)

9 Siân Boyle, 'The sudden rise of AuDHD: What is behind the rocketing rates of this life-changing diagnosis?' *The Guardian*, 4 April 2024, https://www.theguardian.com/lifeandstyle/2024/apr/04/audhd-what-is-behind-rocketing-rates-life-changing-diagnosis?

10 Hussein M. Magdi et al., 'Attention-deficit/hyperactivity disorder and post-traumatic stress disorder adult comorbidity: A systematic review', *Systematic Review Update*, 14(41), (2025), https://doi.org/10.1186/s13643-025-02774-7

11 'Post Traumatic Stress Disorder: Stats and figures', PTSD UK, accessed/modified 6 September 2025, https://www.ptsduk.org/ptsd-stats/

12 Adam Grant, host, Rethinking with Adam Grant, 'Richard Branson on saying yes now and figuring it out later', Apple Podcasts, 18 June 2024, https://podcasts.apple.com/us/podcast/richard-branson-on-saying-yes-now-and-figuring-it-out-later/id1554567118?i=1000659299363

13 Carey Schaal, 'Business: Definition, characteristics & classifications,' Business 101: Principles of Management, Study.com, accessed/modified 21 November 2023, https://study.com/academy/lesson/what-is-a-business-definition-characteristics-examples.html

14 'Pareto Principle', Wikipedia, accessed/modified 3 September 2025, https://en.wikipedia.org/wiki/Pareto_principle

15 Steve Peters, *The Chimp Paradox* (Vermilion, 2012)

16 Emine Saner, 'How the psychology of the England football team could change your life', *The Guardian*, 10 July 2018, https://www.theguardian.com/football/2018/jul/10/psychology-england-football-team-change-your-life-pippa-grange

17 'Habit formation', *Psychology Today*, accessed/modified 3 September 2025, https://www.psychologytoday.com/gb/basics/habit-formation

18 Jamie Laing, host, Great Company with Jamie Laing, 'Part 1 – £200 million to maximum security prison – the insane story of Riordan Maynard', Apple Podcasts, 23 April 2025, https://podcasts.apple.com/nz/podcast/part-1-%C2%A3200-million-to-maximum-security-prison-the/id1735702250?i=1000704524496

19 Joanna Martin, 'Why are females less likely to be diagnosed with ADHD in childhood than males?' *The Lancet Psychiatry*, 11(4), 303–310, https://www.thelancet.com/journals/lanpsy/article/PIIS2215-0366(24)00010-5/fulltext

20 Sam Delaney, 'Ego trap', *The Guardian*, 28 February 2009, https://www.theguardian.com/music/2009/feb/28/bat-for-lashes-beyonce-mariah

21 Caroline Robledo Castro, 'Brief historical review of ADHD and its impact on executive functioning', NeuronUP, 26 February 2024, https://neuronup.us/cognitive-stimulation-news/neurodevelopmental-disorders/adhd/brief-historical-review-of-adhd-and-its-impact-on-executive-functioning/

22 Vania Modesto-Lowe et al., 'Does mindfulness meditation improve attention in attention deficit hyperactivity disorder?', *World Journal of Psychiatry*, 5(4), 397–403 (22 December 2015), https://doi.org/10.5498/wjp.v5.i4.397

23 Erik G. Willcutt et al., 'Validity of the executive function theory of attention-deficit/hyperactivity disorder: A meta-analytic review', *Biological Psychiatry*, 57(11), 1336–1346 (1 June 2005), 10.1016/j.biopsych.2005.02.006

24 Will H. Canu et al., 'Psychometric properties of the Weiss Functional Impairment Rating Scale: Evidence for utility in research, assessment, and treatment of ADHD in emerging adults', *Journal of Attention Disorders*, 24(12), 1648–1660 (October 2020), 10.1177/1087054716661421

25 'Mars Climate Orbiter', NASA Science, accessed/modified 31 August 2025, https://science.nasa.gov/mission/mars-climate-orbiter/

26 'Procrastination', Wikipedia, accessed/modified 31 August 2025, https://en.wikipedia.org/wiki/Procrastination

27 Gloria Mark, 'The cost of interrupted work: More speed and stress', proceedings of ACM CHI 2008 (with Daniela Gudith and Ulrich Klocke), https://ics.uci.edu/~gmark/chi08-mark.pdf

28 Gloria Mark, 'Worker interrupted: The cost of task switching', Fast Company, 28 July 2008, https://www.fastcompany.com/944128/worker-interrupted-cost-task-switching

29 'Menopause', Mayo Clinic, accessed/modified 3 September 2025, https://www.mayoclinic.org/diseases-conditions/menopause/symptoms-causes/syc-20353397#

30 Jeanette Wasserstein et al., '2 perimenopause, menopause and ADHD', *Journal of the International Neuropsychological Society*, 29(s1), 881 (2023), https://www.researchgate.net/publication/376725689_2_Perimenopause_Menopause_and_ADHD

31 William Dodson, 'New insights into rejection sensitive dysphoria', *Additude*, 9 May 2025, https://www.additudemag.com/rejection-sensitive-dysphoria-adhd-emotional-dysregulation/?srsltid=AfmBOoosDFlnNawnnMTRlgJAgFxKF8ABNzErepHCv-LZgMWyYr4QWqSeg

32 'Healing from the fawn trauma response: Reclaiming your voice', Private Therapy Clinic, accessed/modified 3 September 2025, https://theprivatetherapyclinic.co.uk/blog/healing-from-the-fawn-trauma-response/

33 Yaara Turjeman-Levi et al., 'Executive function deficits mediate the relationship between employees' ADHD and job burnout', *AIMS Public Health*, 11(1), 294–314 (12 March 2024), doi: 10.3934/publichealth.2024015

34 Denise C Rogers et al., 'Fatigue in an adult attention deficit hyperactivity disorder population: A trans-diagnostic approach', *British Journal of Clinical Psychology*, 56(1), 33–52 (March 2017), https://pubmed.ncbi.nlm.nih.gov/27918087/

35 'RuPaul explains Drag Race phrase "If you can't love yourself, how are you gonna love somebody else?"', *The Pink News*, 11 September 2024, https://www.thepinknews.com/2024/09/11/rupauls-drag-race-if-you-cant-love-yourself/

36 Katherine Lawton, 'ADHD "sickfluencers" are behind rise in people with self-diagnosed mental health conditions claiming on £69k-a-year disability benefits scheme', *Daily Mail*, 20 January 2025, https://www.dailymail.co.uk/news/article-14303747/ADHD-sickfluencers-rise-self-diagnosed-mental-health-claiming-69k-year.html

Index

INDEX

About the Author

Photograph © Amanda Perry 2026

Amanda Perry is a serial entrepreneur, coach, and speaker who has launched, scaled, and sold four businesses. Her work has been featured in *Forbes, The Guardian*, and on the BBC. She lives in the UK and is passionate about helping ADHD entrepreneurs turn their ideas into thriving, sustainable ventures.

Dear Reader,

We'd love your attention for one more page to tell you about the crisis in children's reading, and what we can all do.

Studies have shown that reading for fun is the **single biggest predictor of a child's future life chances** – more than family circumstance, parents' educational background or income. It improves academic results, mental health, wealth, communication skills, ambition and happiness.[1]

The number of children reading for fun is in rapid decline. Young people have a lot of competition for their time. In 2024, 1 in 10 children and young people in the UK aged 5 to 18 did not own a single book at home.[2]

Hachette works extensively with schools, libraries and literacy charities, but here are some ways we can all raise more readers:

- Reading to children for just 10 minutes a day makes a difference
- Don't give up if children aren't regular readers – there will be books for them!
- Visit bookshops and libraries to get recommendations
- Encourage them to listen to audiobooks
- Support school libraries
- Give books as gifts

There's a lot more information about how to encourage children to read on our website: **www.RaisingReaders.co.uk**

Thank you for reading.

[1] OECD, '21st-Century Readers: Developing Literacy Skills in a Digital World', 2021, https://www.oecd.org/en/publications/21st-century-readers_a83d84cb-en.html

[2] National Literacy Trust, 'Book Ownership in 2024', November 2024, https://literacytrust.org.uk/research-services/research-reports/book-ownership-in-2024